W0246583

STAR WARS

THE ACOLYTE VISUAL GUIDE

STAR WARS

THE ACOLYTE VISUAL GUIDE

WRITTEN BY

PABLO HIDALGO

CONTENTS

FOREWORD

Embarking on a new *Star Wars* journey means being prepared. It means more than just familiarizing yourself with the films of George Lucas, as that's the basic grounding. It means understanding the things that inspired him, and what inspired the storytellers we were lucky enough to work with. In the case of *The Acolyte*, we were fortunate to benefit from decades of experience and passion brought to the fore by people across the entire production. We all brought our love of *Star Wars*.

I met author and lifelong *Star Wars* fan Pablo Hidalgo first in emails and video chats, and then later in person, and we talked about the deepest ramifications of the cosmic and living Force, of balance, and light, dark, dyads, and vergences. It was fascinating. I think I impressed him with the slideshows and documents I created chronicling my thoughts about Osha and Mae and their place in the galaxy.

This book is an encapsulation of all the passion, wisdom, and experience embodied by those who were involved in the creation of *The Acolyte*, under Leslye Headland's leadership. Screenwriters, art directors, prop designers, costume designers, and more channeled their love for the far-away galaxy to tell a new story in this setting. They balanced reverence for what had come before with the courage to blaze new trails and turn new pages. I hope you enjoy it.

Amandla Stenberg,
July 2024

INTRODUCTION TO THE HIGH REPUBLIC

After the defeat of Sith conquerors, the Republic emerges from the ashes of galactic conflict to reach unprecedented heights in the long stretch of peace that follows. It is an era known as the High Republic, and will be remembered as a settled age while the galaxy marches toward a darkening future.

The Jedi Knights serve as guardians of peace and justice, quelling disputes and defeating those who would prey on the helpless. They operate from temples scattered across the Republic, ensuring a direct connection to the civilizations under their protection.

Beneath the surface of this tranquility, danger stirs. Unbeknownst to the Jedi, their enemies—who they thought long vanquished—have survived as a secret chain of masters and apprentices, succeeding one another across the generations while plotting a long vengeance.

After centuries, this threat has faded into myth, all but forgotten as current crises draw the Jedi's attention. However, they remain ever vigilant for signs of disturbance, for any hints of unexpected or unknown manipulations of the Force outside the strictures of their Order.

THE GALAXY OF THE HIGH REPUBLIC ERA

The relative tranquility of the High Republic era allows for an expansion of centralized galactic civilization into the raucous Outer Rim. Much of this enormous region remains unaffiliated, finding a sense of rebellious pride in being "ungovernable." Nonetheless, hundreds of star systems see the benefits of becoming part of a larger community of worlds. While autonomous fiefdoms and coalitions may retain their independence, clusters of Republican constituencies develop on the frontier.

FACTIONS

THE GALACTIC REPUBLIC

Recovered from a calamitous insurrection centuries earlier, the Republic is a democracy presided over by a Senate and chancellor.

THE SITH CONSPIRACY

The Sith survive in the shadows, unknown by the Jedi—who assume them extinct. They carefully calculate their next move.

THE BRENDOK COVEN

In the ancient past of the galaxy, witch covens wielded immense power. Waning in influence, they nonetheless persist.

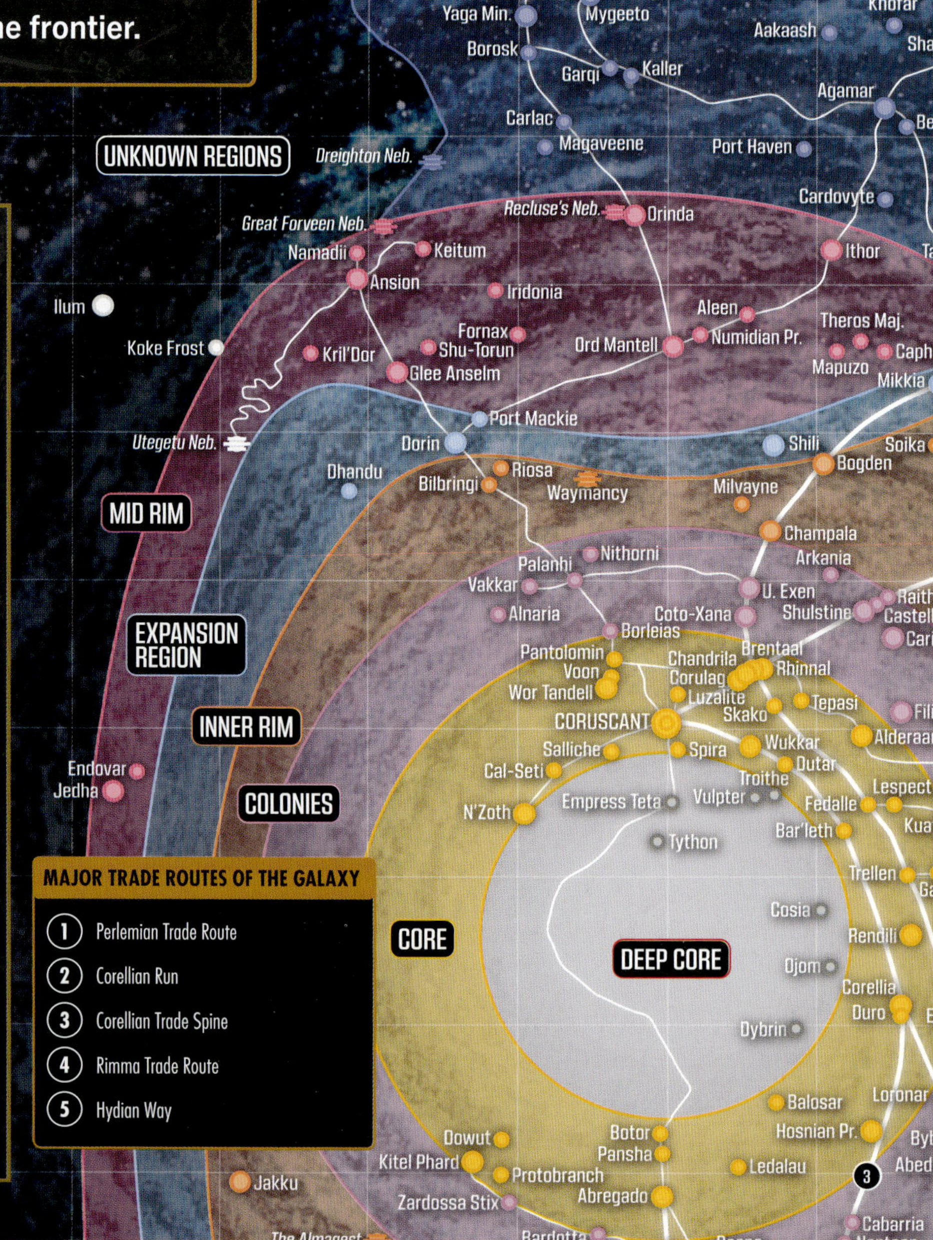

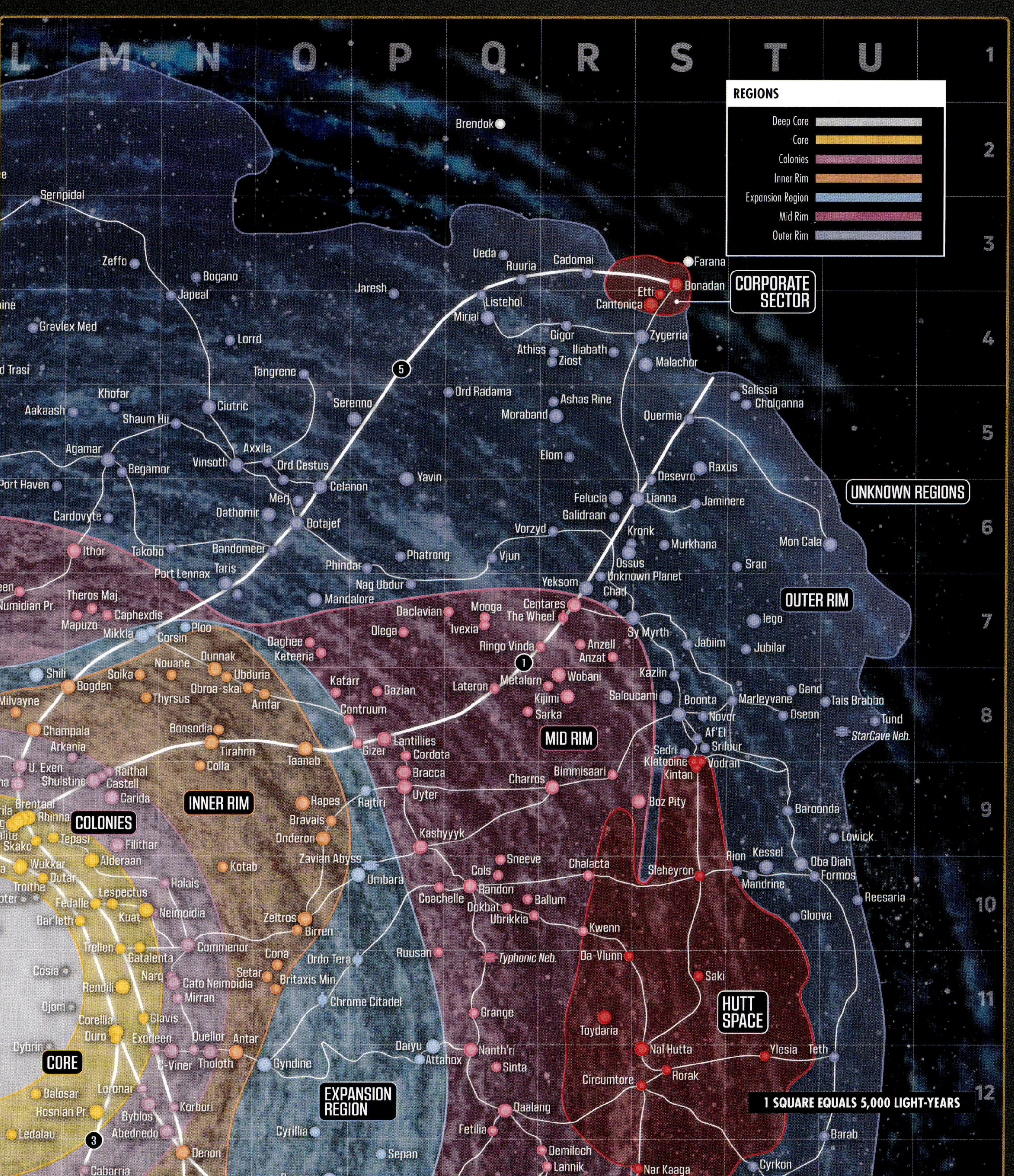
L M N O P Q R S T U
1 2 3 4 5 6 7 8 9 10 11 12
REGIONS
Deep Core
Core
Colonies
Inner Rim
Expansion Region
Mid Rim
Outer Rim
Brendok
Sernpidal
Zeffo
Bogano
Japeal
Gravlex Med
Lorrd
Jaresh
Ueda
Ruuria
Cadomai
Farana
Bonadan
Etti
Cantonica
CORPORATE SECTOR
Listehol
Mirial
Gigor
Athiss
Iliabath
Ziost
Zygerria
Malachor
Tangrene
Khofar
Aakaash
Shaum Hii
Ciutric
Serenno
Ord Radama
Ashas Rine
Moraband
Salissia
Cholganna
Quermia
Agamar
Begamor
Vinsoth
Axxila
Ord Cestus
Elom
Raxus
Desevro
Port Haven
Celanon
Yavin
Felucia
Lianna
Jaminere
UNKNOWN REGIONS
Cardovyte
Merj
Dathomir
Botajef
Galidraan
Vorzyd
Kronk
Murkhana
Ithor
Takobo
Bandomeer
Phatrong
Vjun
Mon Cala
Port Lennax
Taris
Phindar
Ossus
Sran
Nag Ubdur
Unknown Planet
Yeksom
Chad
Theros Maj.
Numidian Pr.
Mandalore
OUTER RIM
Mapuzo
Caphexdis
Daclavian
Mooga
Centares
The Wheel
Iego
Mikkia
Corsin
Ploo
Olega
Ivexia
Sy Myrth
Daghee
Keteeria
Ringo Vinda
Anzell
Anzat
Jabiim
Jubilar
Shili
Soika
Dunnak
Nouane
Ubduria
Bogden
Katarr
Kazlin
Gand
Tais Brabbo
Thyrsus
Obroa-skai
Gazian
Lateron
Metalorn
Wobani
Saleucami
Boonta
Marleyvane
Milvayne
Amfar
Contruum
Kijimi
Sarka
Novor
Oseon
Tund
Champala
Boosodia
MID RIM
Af'El
Sriluur
StarCave Neb.
Arkania
Tirahnn
Taanab
Gizer
Lantillies
Cordota
Sedri
Klatooine
Vodran
U. Exen
Colla
Raithal
Castell
Bracca
Charros
Bimmisaari
Kintan
Shulstine
Carida
Uyter
Boz Pity
INNER RIM
Hapes
Rajtiri
Baroonda
Brentaal
Rhinna
COLONIES
Bravais
Filithar
Tepasi
Skako
Onderon
Kashyyyk
Lowick
Wukkar
Alderaan
Zavian Abyss
Sneeve
Chalacta
Sleheyron
Rion
Kessel
Oba Diah
Dutar
Kotab
Umbara
Cols
Randon
Formos
Troithe
Halais
Mandrine
Lespectus
Coachelle
Dokbat
Ballum
Reesaria
Fedalle
Kuat
Neimoidia
Ubrikkia
Bar'leth
Zeltros
Birren
Kwenn
Gloova
Trellen
Commenor
Gatalenta
Cona
Ruusan
Typhonic Neb.
Da-Vlunn
Narq
Ordo Tera
Setar
Britaxis Min
Saki
Cosia
Cato Neimoidia
Rendili
Mirran
Chrome Citadel
HUTT SPACE
Djom
Glavis
Grange
Toydaria
Corellia
Duro
Exodeen
Quellor
Antar
Dybrin
Tholoth
Daiyu
Nanth'ri
Nal Hutta
Ylesia
Teth
C-Viner
Gyndine
Attahox
CORE
Sinta
Rorak
Circumtore
Lorrd
Balosar
EXPANSION REGION
1 SQUARE EQUALS 5,000 LIGHT-YEARS
Hosnian Pr.
Byblos
Korbori
Daalang
Abednedo
Cyrillia
Fetilia
Barab
Ledalau
Demiloch
Sepan
Cabarria
Denon
Lannik
Nar Kaaga
Cyrkon
Pasaana

THE GALAXY OF THE HIGH REPUBLIC ERA CONTINUED

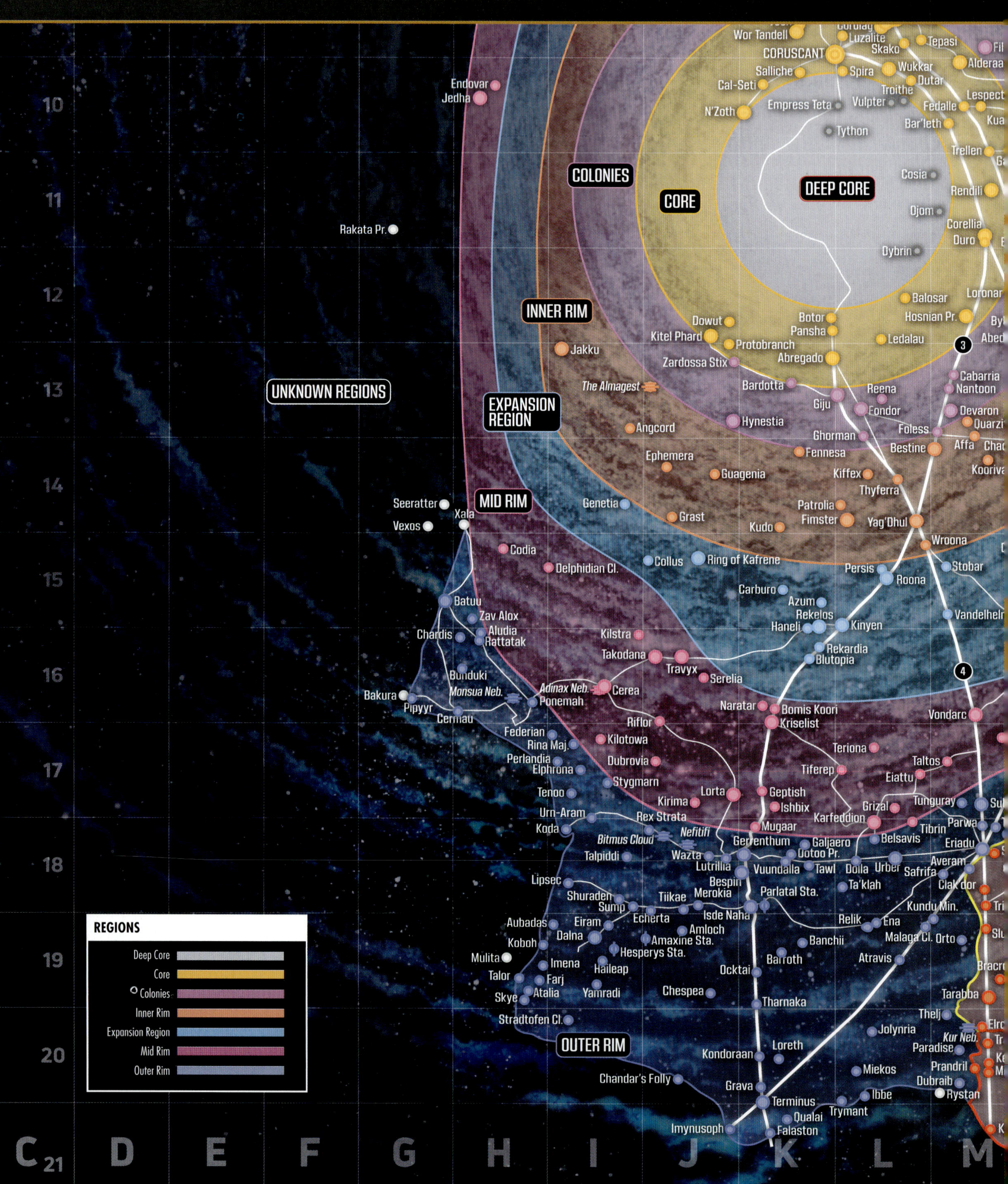

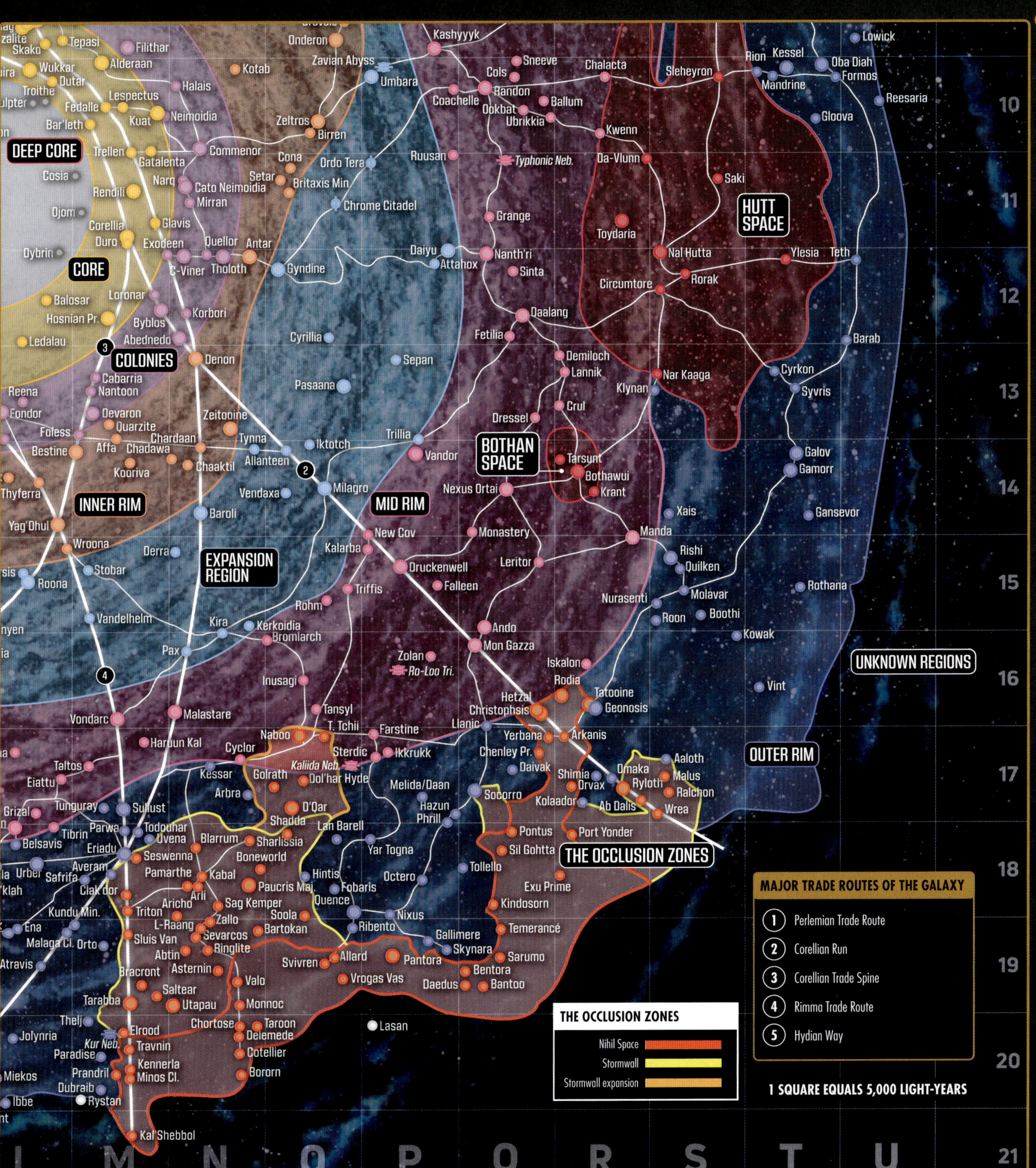
DEEP CORE
CORE
COLONIES
INNER RIM
EXPANSION REGION
MID RIM
BOTHAN SPACE
HUTT SPACE
UNKNOWN REGIONS
OUTER RIM
THE OCCLUSION ZONES
Skako
Tepasi
Filithar
Wukkar
Alderaan
Troithe
Outar
Halais
Lespectus
Fedalle
Kuat
Neimoidia
Bar'leth
Commenor
Trellen
Gatalenta
Cosia
Rendili
Narq
Cato Neimoidia
Mirran
Ojom
Corellia
Glavis
Duro
Exodeen
Quellor
Antar
Dybrin
C-Viner
Tholoth
Loronar
Balosar
Byblos
Korbori
Hosnian Pr.
Abednedo
Ledalau
Denon
Cabarria
Nantoon
Reena
Fondor
Devaron
Quarzite
Zeitooine
Foless
Chardaan
Tynna
Bestine
Affa
Chadawa
Allanteen
Chaaktil
Kooriva
Thyferra
Yag'Dhul
Wroona
Stobar
Roona
Vandelhelm
Derra
Vendaxa
Baroli
Onderon
Kotab
Zavian Abyss
Umbara
Zeltros
Birren
Cona
Ordo Tera
Setar
Britaxis Min.
Chrome Citadel
Gyndine
Cyrillia
Sepan
Pasaana
Iktotch
Milagro
Kashyyyk
Sneeve
Cols
Chalacta
Randon
Coachelle
Ballum
Dokbat
Ubrikkia
Ruusan
Typhonic Neb.
Grange
Daiyu
Attahox
Nanth'ri
Sinta
Qaalang
Fetilia
Demiloch
Lannik
Crul
Dressel
Trillia
Vandor
Tarsunt
Bothawui
Krant
Nexus Ortai
Monastery
New Cov
Kalarba
Leritor
Druckenwell
Falleen
Triffis
Rohm
Kira
Kerkoidia
Bromlarch
Pax
Ando
Mon Gazza
Zolan
Ro-Loo Tri.
Inusagi
Iskalon
Rodia
Sleheyron
Rion
Kessel
Mandrine
Lowick
Oba Diah
Formos
Reesaria
Gloova
Kwenn
Da-Vlunn
Saki
Toydaria
Nal Hutta
Ylesia
Teth
Rorak
Circumtore
Barab
Nar Kaaga
Klynan
Cyrkon
Syvris
Galov
Gamorr
Xais
Gansevor
Manda
Rishi
Quilken
Rothana
Nurasenti
Molavar
Roon
Boothi
Kowak
Vint
Tatooine
Geonosis
Hetzal
Christophsis
Arkanis
Yerbana
Llanic
Chenley Pr.
Daivak
Shimia
Orvax
Omaka
Ryloth
Aaloth
Malus
Ralchon
Kolaador
Ab Dalis
Wrea
Port Yonder
Pontus
Sil Gohtta
Tollello
Exu Prime
Kindosorn
Temerancé
Sarumo
Bentora
Bantoo
Daedus
Pantora
Gallimere
Skynara
Nixus
Ribento
Octero
Yar Togna
Lan Barell
Hazun
Phrill
Melida/Daan
Socorro
Vondarc
Malastare
Harloun Kal
Tansyl
T. Tchii
Farstine
Naboo
Cyclor
Sterdic
Ikkrukk
Kaliida Neb.
Dol'har Hyde
Golrath
Kessar
Arbra
D'Qar
Shadda
Taltos
Eiattu
Grizal
Tunguray
Sullust
Parwa
Todouhar
Uvena
Tibrin
Belsavis
Eriadu
Blarrum
Sharlissia
Seswenna
Boneworld
Averam
Urbel
Safrifa
Pamarthe
Kabal
Hintis
Fobaris
Quence
Paucris Maj.
Clak'dor
Arli
Aricho
Sag Kemper
Kundu Min.
Triton
Zallo
Soola
L-Raang
Sevarcos
Bartokan
Ena
Malaga Cl.
Sluis Van
Orto
Ringlite
Abtin
Allard
Svivren
Atravis
Bracront
Asternin
Vrogas Vas
Valo
Saltear
Tarabba
Utapau
Monnoc
Thelj
Chortose
Taroon
Delemede
Jolynria
Elrood
Kur Neb.
Travnin
Cotellier
Paradise
Kennerla
Prandril
Minos Cl.
Boronn
Miekos
Dubraib
Ibbe
Rystan
Kal'Shebbol
Lasan
L
M
N
O
P
Q
R
S
T
U
10
11
12
13
14
15
16
17
18
19
20
21
THE OCCLUSION ZONES
Nihil Space
Stormwall
Stormwall expansion
MAJOR TRADE ROUTES OF THE GALAXY
1 Perlemian Trade Route
2 Corellian Run
3 Corellian Trade Spine
4 Rimma Trade Route
5 Hydian Way
1 SQUARE EQUALS 5,000 LIGHT-YEARS

CHAPTER 1

THE FIRST TARGET

Jedi Master Indara is operating out of distant Ueda when she becomes Mae Aniseya's first target. The assignment: the killing of a Jedi, executed without a weapon. Only the completion of such an impossibility will prove to Mae's mysterious master that she has the cunning and power to become his acolyte. Mae, a stranger to this world, boldly confronts the Jedi.

UEDA

Ueda is a relatively new signatory into the Galactic Republic, having been incorporated within the last 80 standard years. It is not part of a formal sector in the Outer Rim, an expanse still largely independent of Republic representation. Ueda was the site of lucrative logging and milling operations, as the northern archipelagos are a source of the durable and valuable Ueda conifer. In the past, marauders would strike the planet for its processed materials.

GATES OF THE CITY

The gates mark the entrance to Point Ueda, the capital city of the planet. Once the site of the administrative offices for the logging operations, the settlement was also where the mill workers lived. As trade grew, so the population diversified.

Lodging and hospitality quarter

Old Loggers' Hill cemetery

Causeway made from sunken parapet wall

HIGH REPUBLIC CREDITS

Several currencies can be spent freely in Point Ueda, including the Republic credit standard (also known as the datary). Older coinage is common, as opposed to the more modern gleaming ingots produced by minting worlds.

Bosphian sestertius

Republic datary

DATA FILE

REGION Outer Rim

SECTOR Unincorporated Bosphian provinces

SYSTEM Ueda

DIAMETER 14,339 km (8,910 miles)

TERRAIN Forested island chains

MOONS 1 (Uedar)

POPULATION 24.3 million

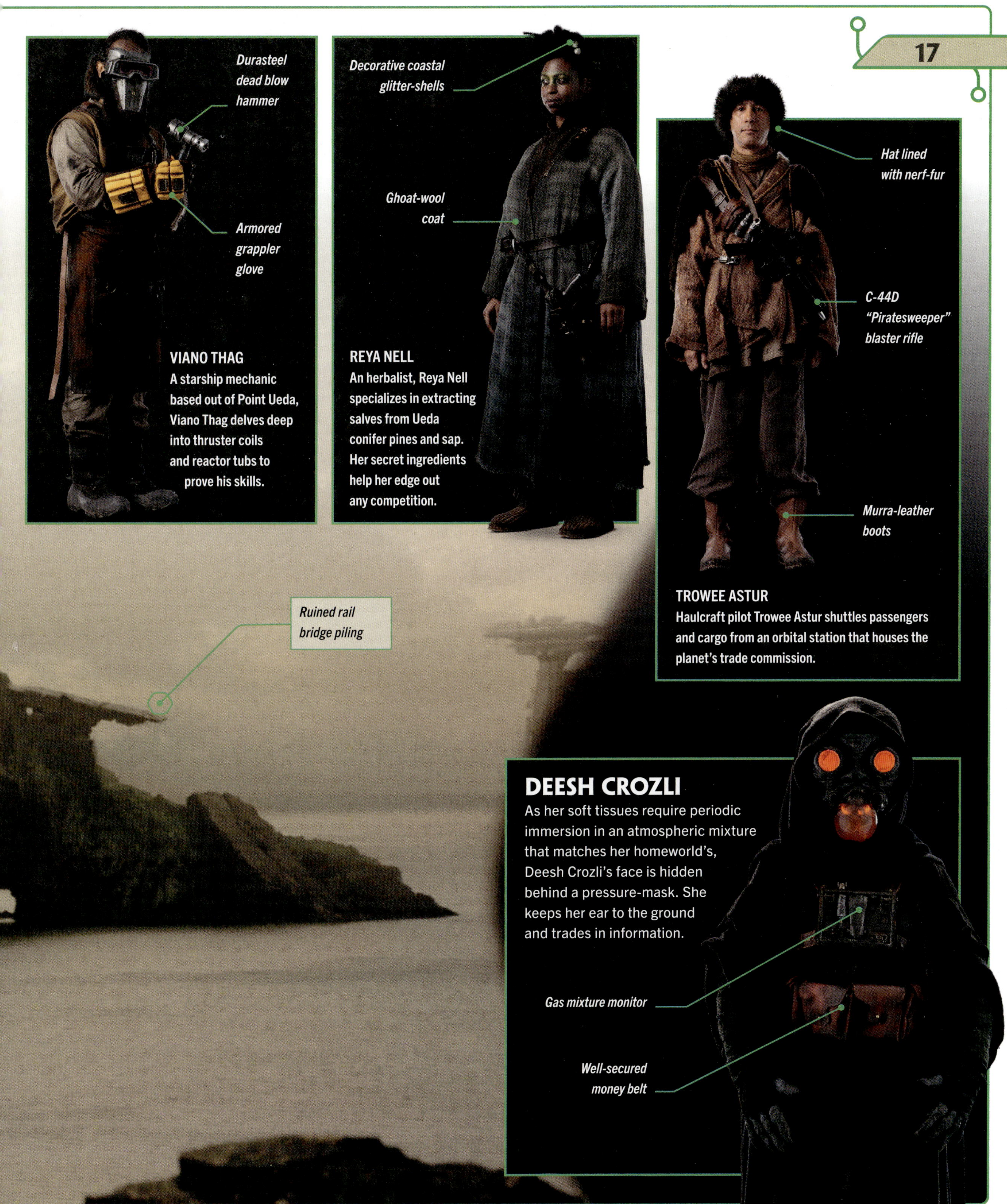

VIANO THAG
A starship mechanic based out of Point Ueda, Viano Thag delves deep into thruster coils and reactor tubs to prove his skills.

REYA NELL
An herbalist, Reya Nell specializes in extracting salves from Ueda conifer pines and sap. Her secret ingredients help her edge out any competition.

TROWEE ASTUR
Haulcraft pilot Trowee Astur shuttles passengers and cargo from an orbital station that houses the planet's trade commission.

DEESH CROZLI

As her soft tissues require periodic immersion in an atmospheric mixture that matches her homeworld's, Deesh Crozli's face is hidden behind a pressure-mask. She keeps her ear to the ground and trades in information.

UEDA NOODLE SHOP

The Lomi Usqi Noodle Shop is named after a previous owner from more than 160 years ago. The shop's sign has faded beyond legibility, and locals simply call it "the Noodle Shop," as it's the only establishment of its kind in Point Ueda. It is a tired, two-story structure made of some of the oldest timbers in town, and has served multiple roles in the settlement's long history—including as an inn and a town hall in its earliest days. Cabuck, the current manager and bartender, has stocked the bar with more than broth, so it's become a welcoming public house for travelers and locals alike.

Mae Aniseya strides boldly into the shop, past the hungry and convivial diners, and approaches the table occupied by her target. Jedi Master Indara sits with some locals, bemused by the masked stranger who demands combat. Terse words are exchanged and violence erupts when Mae batters Indara's compatriots, spurring the Jedi into action. Sensing there's more to this altercation, patrons begin to flee.

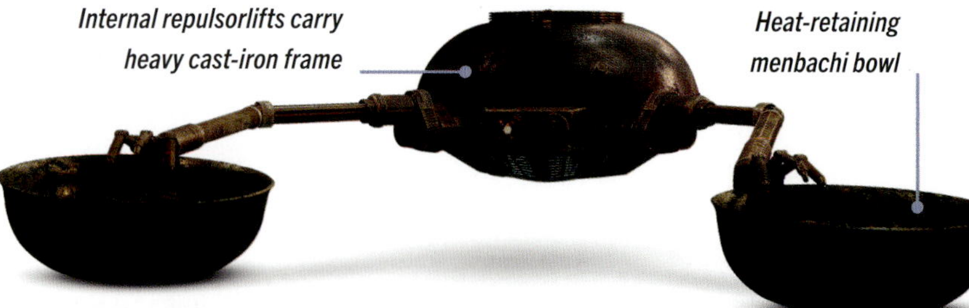

K7-1EG

A cranky server droid, K7-1EG is cobbled together from pieces of other droids and kitchen appliances. Overworked and undermaintained, "Wuniji" is the butt of many cruel jokes from churlish regulars.

Wuniji's processors calculate and recheck estimates for Kesmer Faloodi's appetite.

MIOW JOON

The burly Miow Joon keeps the circular noodle-drying rack spinning, spacing out the edible strands to prevent them from clumping. Nicknamed the Noodle Peddler, Joon is overqualified for the job; he is a champion velospeeder rider who comes to Ueda during his training seasons. In exchange for a space to work out and free food packed with carbohydrates, he offers his muscular service.

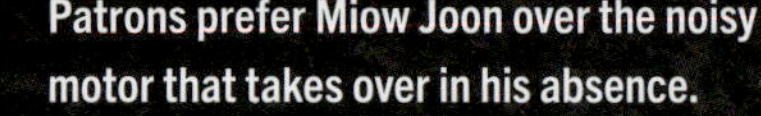

Patrons prefer Miow Joon over the noisy motor that takes over in his absence.

KELLA ANTRO

From a chilly coastal town, salt trader Kella Antro supports her aging parents by delivering seasoning minerals to the noodle shop. She chose the wrong day to visit when she is held at knifepoint by Mae and then thrown from the second-floor balcony to distract Indara, who rescues Kella.

Family crest woven into heirloom overcoat

KESMER FALOODI

A charming gossip, Kesmer Faloodi hoodwinks visitors into covering his bill and can go days without paying for a meal. He is unaware that his "Bottomless" nickname refers to his gluttonous appetite.

NOODLE SHOP CHOPSTICKS

BIHUN AND BASKO

Wrosidians are semi-plant-based life-forms that start life as buds on a singular stalk. This reproduction method has led Wrosidian culture to have no direct equivalents of familial or gender identities when compared to most other galactic communities. Bihun (left) and Basko (right) are "relatives" from the same stalk but are not exactly siblings.

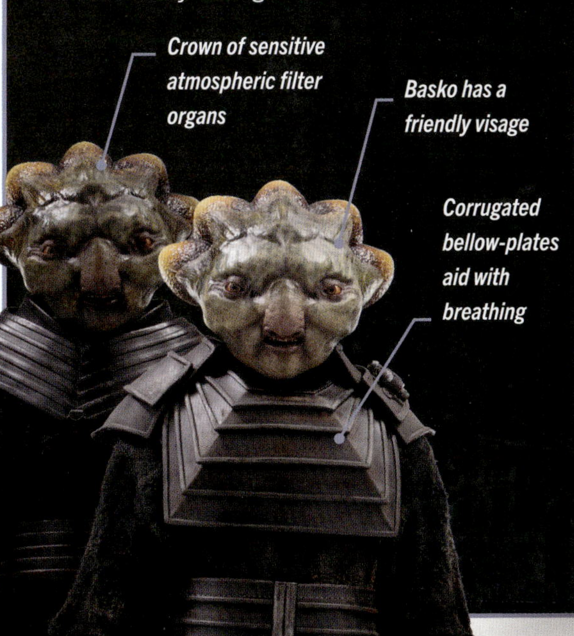

CABUCK AND JUNIOR

Cabuck, the current proprietor, has resisted naming or overly customizing the noodle shop out of superstition, as he believes Lomi Usqi haunts the premises. Cabuck is a Drezar with wide-set eyes that allow him to attend to multiple guests while watching out for his young son.

Secret spices shaker

Calloused skin toughened from lifetime of kitchen work

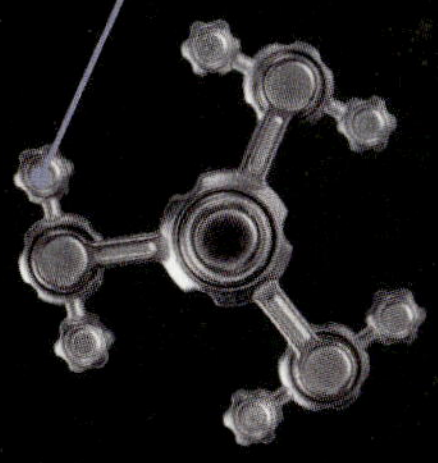

Repurposed tankage seal

JUNIOR'S SPINNER TOY

Cabuck Junior, shy 3-year-old

DATA FILE

SUBJECT Cabuck

HOMEWORLD Drez

SPECIES Drezar

AFFILIATION Ueda Noodle Shop

HEIGHT 1.93 m (6 ft 4 in)

AGE 34 standard years

MAE ANISEYA

Driven by vengeance and a hunger for power that will protect her from loss, Mae Aniseya has struck a devilish bargain with a mysterious mentor. The Stranger's promise is to hone her natural abilities and to make her an acolyte. To prove her mettle, Aniseya must do the seemingly impossible: to kill a Jedi, but to do so without a weapon. To that end, Aniseya has been perfecting her innate skills through rigorous training. She is a lithe, silent assassin who can burst forward with intense physical power, calling upon the Force to give her a deadly edge.

Mae's targets are four Jedi who visited her home planet of Brendok 16 years earlier, bringing with them death and destruction. From her personal perspective, the Jedi encounter resulted in her home ablaze, her people dead, and her twin sister vanished. Time and anger have concentrated this point of view into a searing memory that drives her into murderous action. She begins her vendetta on Ueda, where the Jedi Master Indara is her first target.

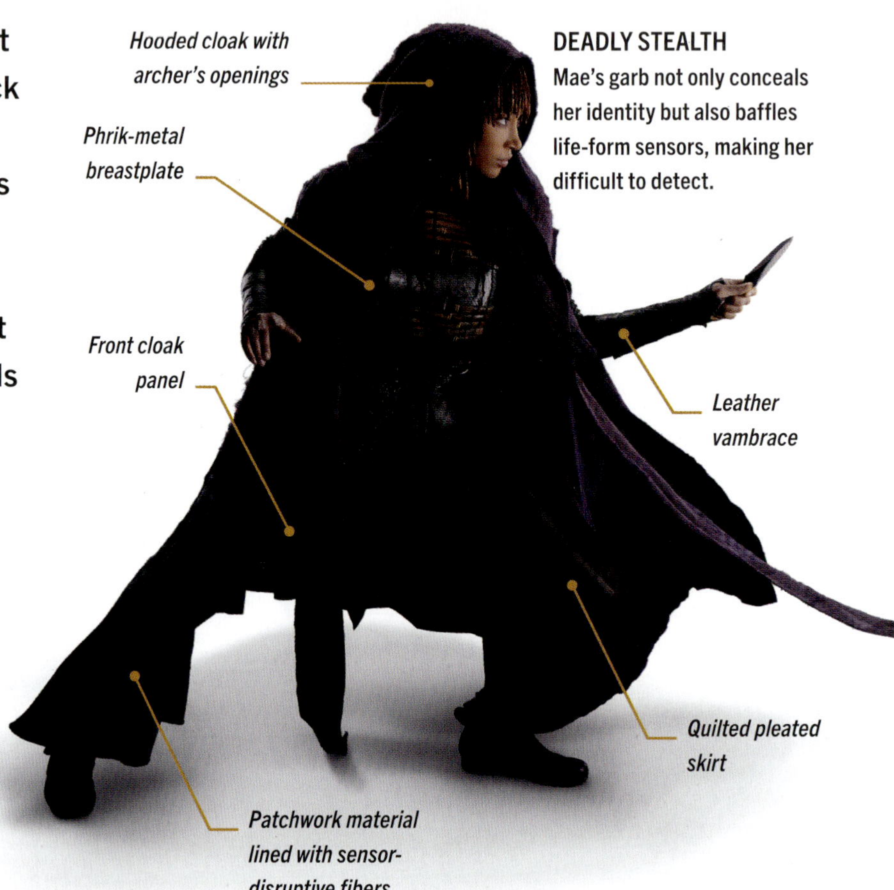

DEADLY STEALTH
Mae's garb not only conceals her identity but also baffles life-form sensors, making her difficult to detect.

"WE HAVE UNFINISHED BUSINESS. ATTACK ME WITH ALL YOUR STRENGTH."

MAE ANISEYA TO MASTER INDARA

TIMELINE

Age 8	Mae undergoes the Ascension ceremony on Brendok, completing the ritual under a lunar eclipse and bearing the mark of the coven. Tragedy strikes, and Mae is left alone.
Age 22	After years of drifting, Mae meets Qimir and his secretive master, who begins to train her in deadly arts. They will eventually strike a deal.
Age 24	Mae begins to fulfill her bargain with the mysterious master, attempting to kill a Jedi without a weapon.

MAE'S SUPPLY BAG

MAE'S SATCHEL

ASSASSIN'S ESSENTIALS

Mae travels light to give her the mobility required for swift escapes. Her larger expedition supply bag is for extended journeys, such as her trek through the Khofar forests. The smaller satchel is an all-purpose go-bag with travel basics, like Republic dataries and falsified identification.

RELENTLESS VENDETTA

Supernatural talents would ordinarily atrophy with age and lack of formal practice, but Mae has undertaken an intense regimen of focusing her rage over the past two years, tempering dark anger into a precisely controlled weapon. She adopts a formality as she approaches her quarry, identifying her target by name and demanding that they attack her. Tactically, she attempts to disarm them to level the advantages in combat.

DATA FILE

SUBJECT Mae Aniseya

HOMEWORLD Brendok

SPECIES Human

AFFILIATION Formerly Brendoki Force-witch coven; currently independent

HEIGHT 1.67 m (5 ft 6 in)

AGE 24 standard years

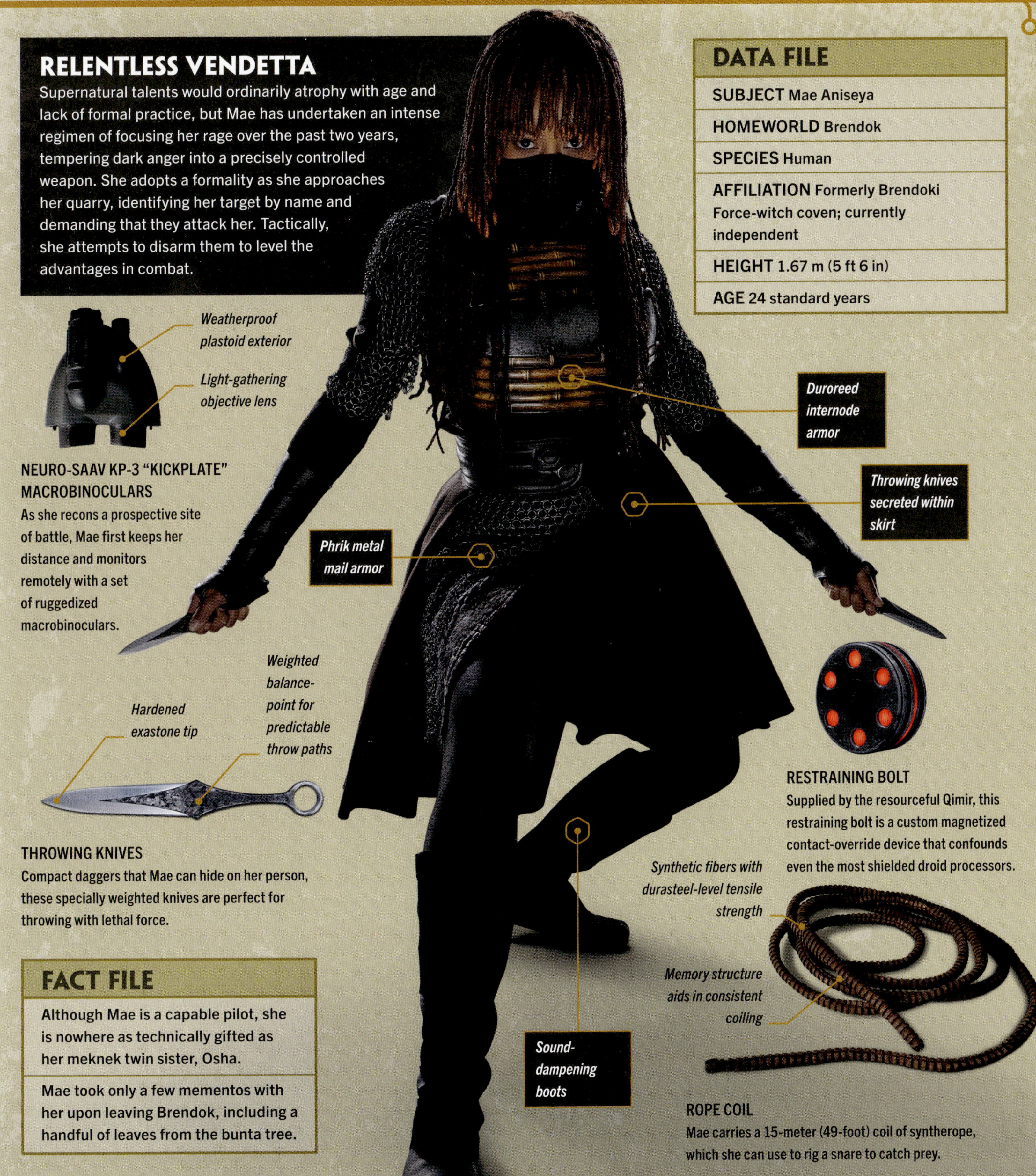

NEURO-SAAV KP-3 "KICKPLATE" MACROBINOCULARS

As she recons a prospective site of battle, Mae first keeps her distance and monitors remotely with a set of ruggedized macrobinoculars.

THROWING KNIVES

Compact daggers that Mae can hide on her person, these specially weighted knives are perfect for throwing with lethal force.

RESTRAINING BOLT

Supplied by the resourceful Qimir, this restraining bolt is a custom magnetized contact-override device that confounds even the most shielded droid processors.

ROPE COIL

Mae carries a 15-meter (49-foot) coil of syntherope, which she can use to rig a snare to catch prey.

FACT FILE

Although Mae is a capable pilot, she is nowhere as technically gifted as her meknek twin sister, Osha.

Mae took only a few mementos with her upon leaving Brendok, including a handful of leaves from the bunta tree.

MASTER INDARA

Master Indara's duties on Ueda usually have her interacting with planetary leaders, local marshals, and civic representatives, to ensure that peace and fairness are kept in what can otherwise be a riotous setting. Though such diplomacy takes up most of her time, she much prefers the more grounded atmosphere of the Point Ueda noodle shop, and hearing from local traders and passers-through to get unvarnished truths and agenda-free reports of what's really going on.

Indara has long been a "Jedi of the people," undergoing a break from Temple duty to spend some time as a Wayseeker. For this practice, she communed with the Force and learned from the galaxy at large through face-to-face explorations of worlds and populations. Among the unique experiences this gave her was the study of various forms of martial arts. She became a pupil under several masters of other traditions. Her humble acts enriched her own appreciation of the Jedi arts. She has taken this knowledge and augmented her already impressive combat skills.

Indara at age 38, during the mission to Brendok

Standard Jedi utility belt

Field mission robes

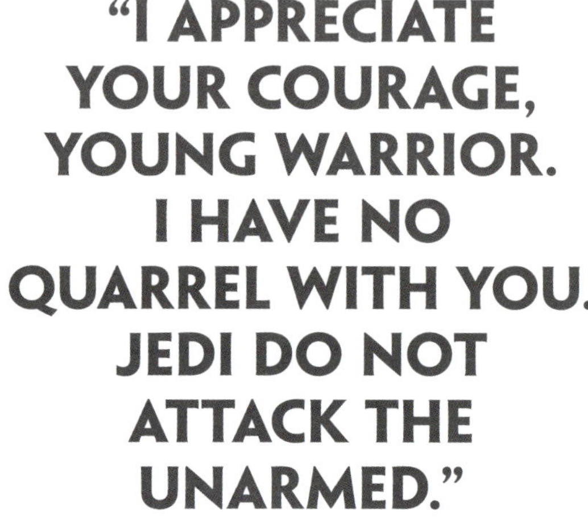

"I APPRECIATE YOUR COURAGE, YOUNG WARRIOR. I HAVE NO QUARREL WITH YOU. JEDI DO NOT ATTACK THE UNARMED."

MASTER INDARA TO MAE ANISEYA

THE INDARA LESSONS

Indara's wide-ranging travels to learn esoteric and exotic martial arts forms from varied masters has enriched her understanding of her connection to the Force. She has recorded summaries of her experiences in a holocron that is frequently checked out of the Jedi Temple library by curious Padawans looking to expand their defensive skills.

LOBEREKI

A courier with a fast ship, Lobereki's frequent travels keep him informed of any nearby incidents worth reporting to Indara. He admires the Jedi greatly and finds her somewhat attractive, for a non-Duraceph.

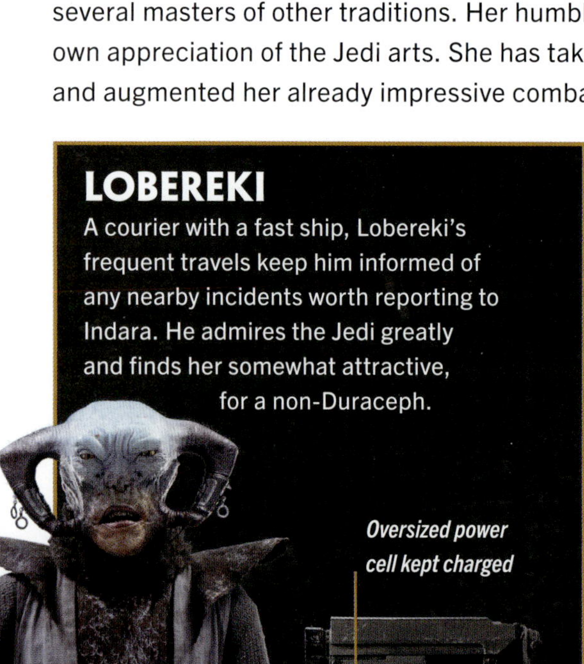

Oversized power cell kept charged

LOBEREKI'S BLASTER

Rarely used blaster tends to stick in holster

OHAL ALOND

A repulsor-barge captain who ferries a variety of goods to and from Point Ueda, Ohal Alond is a shrewd negotiator. He is a seasoned pazaak player who sets aside a portion of his earnings for gambling.

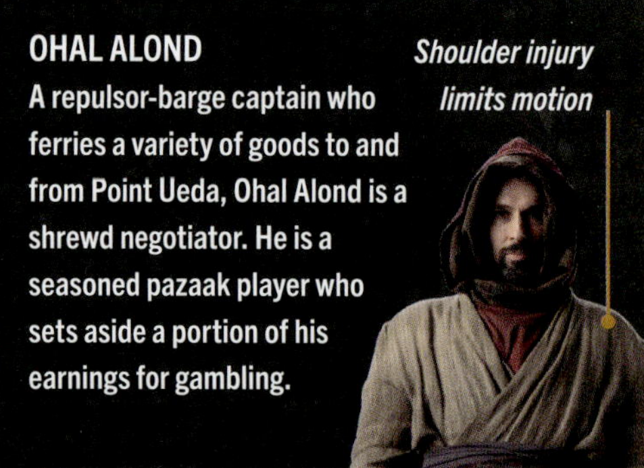

Shoulder injury limits motion

TIANRIS MEZ

Along with his Clarodian brother Guanlos, Tianris Mez supervises a mining operation but is looking to retire soon. He doesn't think his younger sibling can handle the responsibility, and often asks Indara for advice and wisdom.

Simple spun-moss cloak

GUANLOS MEZ

Guanlos Mez is a miner on Ueda, supervising an old family deep-mantle operation in the Eastern Wilderness. He enjoys a crude joke and the novelty that the local Jedi also engages in colorful banter.

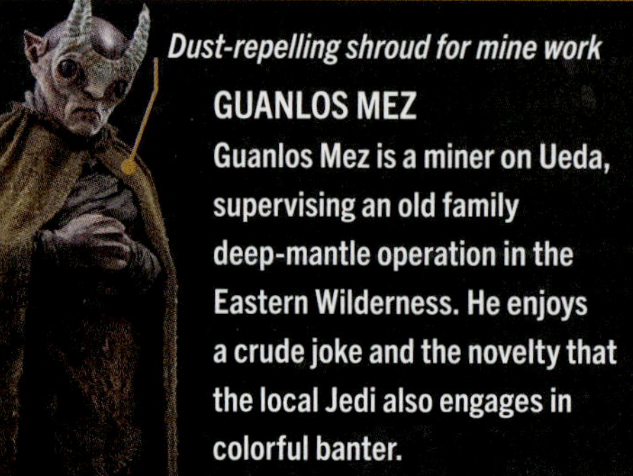

Dust-repelling shroud for mine work

DYN PILGA

In the summers, Pilga works as a lumberjack clearing out overgrowth from the coastal forests, and in the winters he is a trapper keeping the pinedriller population under control. He feels protective of Ueda's environment.

Pinedriller wool hat

TIMELINE

Age 25	Reaches Knighthood but shifts focus to archival duties following the abrupt death of her master.
Age 26	Becomes a Wayseeker after working with and learning directly from Vernestra Rwoh.
Age 28	Returns to Jedi Temple after earning Skoydon marking. Begins training Padawan Torbin.
Age 38	Exploration mission to Brendok, which results in Osha Aniseya's entrance into the Jedi Order.
Age 40	Undergoes another stint as a Wayseeker and earns second Skoydon marking.
Age 43	Welcomed back to the Jedi Temple.
Age 52	Commences posting at Ueda.
Age 54	Confronted and killed by a mysterious attacker at Point Ueda.

GRACE, POWER, WISDOM

With decades of experience and possessing many useful traits, Indara is a shining example of Jedi excellence. She can wield great power in combat, but it is deployed with graceful precision and no wasted effort. More importantly, she knows when not to fight—when to keep her blade unignited.

Synth-leather chestpiece with hook-and-bar spinal closure

Power cell charge indicators

INDARA'S LIGHTSABER
With a sensible copper finish and an emitter shroud denoting caution, Indara's lightsaber reflects her well.

FACT FILE

During her Wayseeker years, Indara studied the Skoydon school of martial arts intensively, earning two markings several years apart, which adorn her temple next to her left eye.

Other fighting disciplines Indara is adept at include Sera Plinck, Bakuuni Hand, Gravik-nez, Wrruushi (as taught by Kelnacca), and Zavat.

DATA FILE

SUBJECT Indara

HOMEWORLD Coruscant

SPECIES Human

AFFILIATION Jedi Order

HEIGHT 1.77 m (5 ft 9 in)

AGE 54 standard years

Billowing robes can help obscure stance to confound opponents

Brilliant green-bladed lightsaber from crystal gathered on Ilum

LIFE IN THE CORPORATE SECTOR

A distant sector of space set aside for unrestrained commercial exploitation, the Corporate Sector (CorpSec) is a fiefdom devoted to profit. A negotiated treaty with the Republic stipulates that CorpSec cannot develop on any worlds with preexisting intelligent life. Financial growth has given the independent sector increasing political power, and its borders have grown since its original inception.

Deflector shield projector

Service ports lead to access tunnels

Static discharge vanes

CAPTAIN BLEX

The Neimoidian captain of the *Fallon*, Blex is falling behind his revenue requirements with the quarterly deadline looming over his well-adorned head. Blex cuts corners where he can to ensure a profitable run. The interception of his ship by a Jedi Vector sees credits and stock options evaporating before his eyes.

FACT FILE

- Captain Blex desperately desires promotion onto a larger class of ship with more profitable hauls.
- A stress ulcer irritating Blex's lung pods leads to frequent exasperated sighs.

Captain's campanulate hat with folded crown

Aromatically infused collar

Concealed sonic stunner for self-defense

Tiered epaulet

Draped cloak of command

DATA FILE

MANUFACTURER Hoersch-Kessel Drive Inc.

MODEL WD-2250 *Whydah*-class Yield Conveyer

TYPE Freighter

DIMENSIONS Height: 91.48 m (300 ft); Length: 259.27 m (850 ft 6 in); Width: 77.54 m (254 ft 4 in)

SPEED 85 megalight per hour; Atmospheric: 975 kph (606 mph)

WEAPONS 2 forward defensive laser cannons

AFFILIATION Trade Federation

FALLON

The *Fallon's* long frame forms a shell protecting suspended cargo modules that are magnetically attached to the ship's superstructure. A total of 24 standardized containers, four medium tanks, and one large tank provide varied stowage for valuable goods. The ship is lightly armed, relying on the security of CorpSec.

Outrigging engineering section to clear space for cargo

Reinforced hull with acceleration compensator field projectors

Magnacleats to attach additional cargo netting

"TO WHAT DO WE OWE THE PLEASURE OF JEDI PRESENCE ON OUR HUMBLE SHIP?"

CAPTAIN BLEX TO YORD FANDAR

KEY CORPORATE SECTOR SIGNATORIES

The Corporate Sector sprang from the efforts of the Galactic Corporate Policy League, a lobbying group that was able to secure the support of key senators. Notable charter members include:

TRADE FEDERATION Interstellar shipping and trade consortium led from Cato Neimoidia.

TAGGE COMPANY Mining and heavy manufacturing concern located on Tepasi.

CONSOLIDATED HOLDINGS OF PRE-OX MORLANA CORPORATION Multi-industry conglomerate based out of the Xappyh sector.

KUAT DRIVE YARDS (KDY) Major starship design house operating from Kuat.

CHIEWAB AMALGAMATED PHARMACEUTICAL COMPANY Medical and chemical conglomerate with notable exploratory fleet.

CYBOT GALACTICA Major droid manufacturer established on Affa.

CHIEF OFFICER QUEYA

An ambitious Neimoidian merchant fleet officer, Queya is disappointed by Blex's lack of foresight and strategy. She helps to cover his missteps until she can secure promotion or a transfer to a different vessel.

First Mate's command hat

Silver trim denotes rank

Posture for secret gestural Pak Pak language

Velvoid with crushed pile finish

OSHA ANISEYA

Osha Aniseya is far more than an interstellar meknek crawling atop starship hulls and within the innards of propulsion systems. She harbors a veiled past and an unhealed emotional wound of a childhood accident that tore her life apart.

The staunch advocacy of Master Sol carved out the exception that allowed Osha entry into Jedi training at an advanced age. Her mind had already been opened to feeling and manipulating the Force, and Sol argued that the Jedi had a responsibility to the orphaned girl. The backing of Master Indara's influential voice convinced an otherwise cautious Jedi Council to proceed with her training.

Despite the best efforts of Sol and Osha, and an undeniably strong bond forged between master and Padawan apprentice, the training failed. Osha chose to leave the Order, unable to fortify her focus against loss, feeling as if an essential part of her was unaccounted for.

She wandered the Outer Rim directionless before settling into the boisterous life of a meknek, stitching together a network of friends and contacts. In private, Osha still thinks of matters left unfinished.

Pivoting actinic work lamp

Reinforced breathing hose

OSHA'S MEKNEK HELMET

Vital gasses status display indicator

Replaceable alga-scrubber convertor tube

TRAVELING LIGHT

As meknek life is itinerant, moving from ship to ship with little notice, Osha has few possessions. Aside from her faithful PIP droid, most of her basic gear fits in a simple backpack. Her hasty departure from Brendok separated her from all trappings of her childhood, and her frugal life as a Jedi left her with no belongings.

Water bottle with integrated purifier

OUTFITTED MEKNEK

Meknek is a Huttese word for a profession they originated long ago: cheap labor as starship mechanics in exchange for lodging aboard a host vessel. The Hutts, ever eager to demonstrate superiority, took pride in the number of thralls they had under their command willing to risk life for their whims. With the advent of astromech technology, mekneks are now seen as an uncivilized throwback, or a crude cultural leftover. Meknek use is still prevalent in the Outer Rim and especially in Hutt Space.

TIMELINE

Age 8	Osha is to undergo the Ascension ceremony on Brendok that would elevate her to leadership of a Force-witch coven. Tragedy strikes, and Osha survives to be taken into the Jedi Order.
Age 18	Her inability to focus beyond her loss hampers Osha's training and she leaves the Jedi Order.
Age 24	Osha is intercepted by the Jedi for suspicion of murder, an act corroborated by an eyewitness.

OSHA

As a child, Osha demonstrates a questing curiosity for what lies beyond Brendok and the technology that pervades the galaxy. She has an analytical nature and a knack for breaking down tangled designs to their base shapes, something evident in her childhood sketchbooks. Her days as a Padawan exposed her to modern devices, preparing her for the meknek life.

"LEAVING THE JEDI WAS THE HARDEST THING I'VE EVER DONE, BUT IT WAS MY DECISION. NO ONE ELSE'S."

OSHA ANISEYA TO YORD FANDAR

Color-coding for batch helps track freshness

Cost of ration is deducted from meknek pay

SEALED NUTRISTICK

Mekneks grab meals when they can, and Osha has acquired a taste for sealed protein-dense nutristicks.

Personal monitor for radiation and hazardous field exposure

Holster is a charging cradle

Insulated gloves, fingerless for sensitive tactile work

FACT FILE

Osha has a meknek tattoo on her upper arm from a raucous night of partying on Etti IV.

Without constant mental exercise and focused training, Osha's Jedi abilities have gradually faded over the last six years.

Reinforced work pants with multiple tool pockets

DATA FILE

SUBJECT Osha Aniseya

HOMEWORLD Brendok

SPECIES Human

AFFILIATION Formerly Brendoki Force-witch coven; formerly Jedi Order; current meknek

HEIGHT 1.67 m (5 ft 6 in)

AGE 24 standard years

PIP

Found in workshops across the galaxy, the PIP unit is a versatile tool essential to mekneks. Pui-ui Implement Products developed a range of PIP units that embody a flexible repair philosophy. Though droids perform an increasingly large percentage of menial repair tasks, there is still a need for expert living technicians that bring an organic's discerning judgment and experience.

Living techs are able to customize repair solutions that are specific to the moment, to the owner's needs, and within a budget, taking into account the unique history of the problematic equipment. In these instances, a PIP unit enhances an organic technician rather than replaces them. Osha Aniseya personalizes her PIP droid as "Pip," as she takes the uncommon habit of addressing it directly by a familiar name.

"OH, THIS IS A PIP DROID. I'M TRYING TO SYNC INTO YOUR SHIP SO I CAN GET SOME FUEL LEVELS AND SOME VITALS..."
OSHA ANISEYA TO MASTER SOL

OSHA'S WORKBENCH

PIP units have standardized interfaces so they can be charged through common ports and connected to starship diagnostic networks. Workbenches like the one on the *Fallon* have a variety of PIP-compatible body frames that the cognitive unit can connect with. Adaptive software bridges programming differences between the PIP and ship.

Field calibrator base with degausser wand

Osha's "Pip" plugged into docking cradle

Table-mounted illuminated magnifier unit

Trade Federation iconography

OSHA'S PIP

Osha's PIP unit seems expressive and friendly, but it is largely imitative behavior learned from Osha's tenderness toward the device. To what degree Pip is "aware" is something for droid theorists to debate, but Osha treats "him" as a close and trusted friend, something she swears results in a more reliable performance.

Plate conceals welder extension

Wireless communications antenna

Filtered photoreceptor slots

Tool carousel window

FACT FILE

Osha has personalized her preferred PIP body frame with chassisplast stickers.

Pip's "personality" resides in the head module. Interfacing with a strange body chassis requires frequent virus checks.

Variable gauge head

BIT-DRIVER MODE
Pip's head becomes a handheld bit-driver once the shank extends from its rotating base.

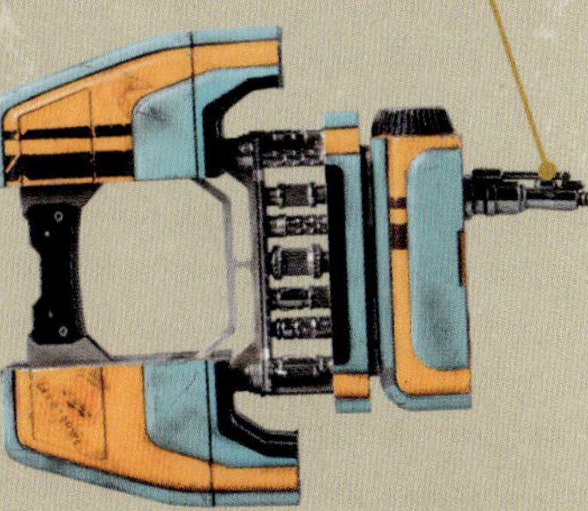

Vacuum-synergic welding head

WELDER MODE
The split-body configuration offers stability when deploying the welding head for delicate and accurate work.

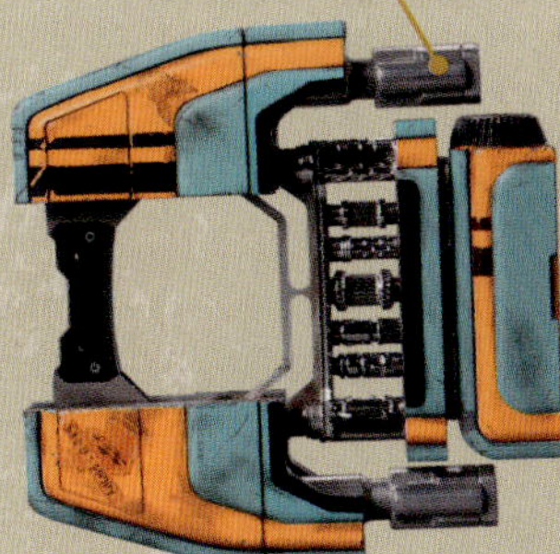

Compressed nonconductive pyro-suppressant chemical nozzle

FIRE EXTINGUISHER MODE
Splitting the body frame reveals a stable single-hand grip so Pip can be aimed accurately.

DATA FILE

MANUFACTURER Pui-ui Implement Products

TYPE Personal multitool repair assistant

HEIGHT 18 cm (7 in) with neck extended

WEAPONS None

AFFILIATION Meknek

MEKNEK LIFE

There are few jobs more dangerous than that of a meknek, though this desperate trade has accrued its own rich strain of fanciful folklore, where the numerous risks are glossed over. The term "meknek" has evolved over the centuries in relation to the risky profession. In the current era, it specifically describes a type of worker who trades mechanical skills for room and board on traveling ships, living out an itinerant existence among the stars.

The Republic has outlawed the practice in most regions, due to the dangers involved and for its exploitative nature. According to one strict Huttese tradition, workers are never able to escape the dangerous trade. In the Corporate Sector, the Trade Federation can sidestep regulations for cheap labor.

FOREMAN DROID

J09-4MN is a repurposed Veril Line Systems repair droid that dispenses work assignments and monitors billable work hours. The droid keeps an active telemetric diagnostic link to each of the meknek spacesuits.

Primary sensor cluster

Gravity-adjusting feet

MEKNEK OSHA

After leaving the Jedi Order, 18-year-old Osha Aniseya needed to find work, and after a few misadventures, she signed up with a meknek crew in Hutt Space. She was one of the few to escape the Hutt-controlled space lanes, finding various berths aboard independent vessels before securing an under-the-table CorpSec contract.

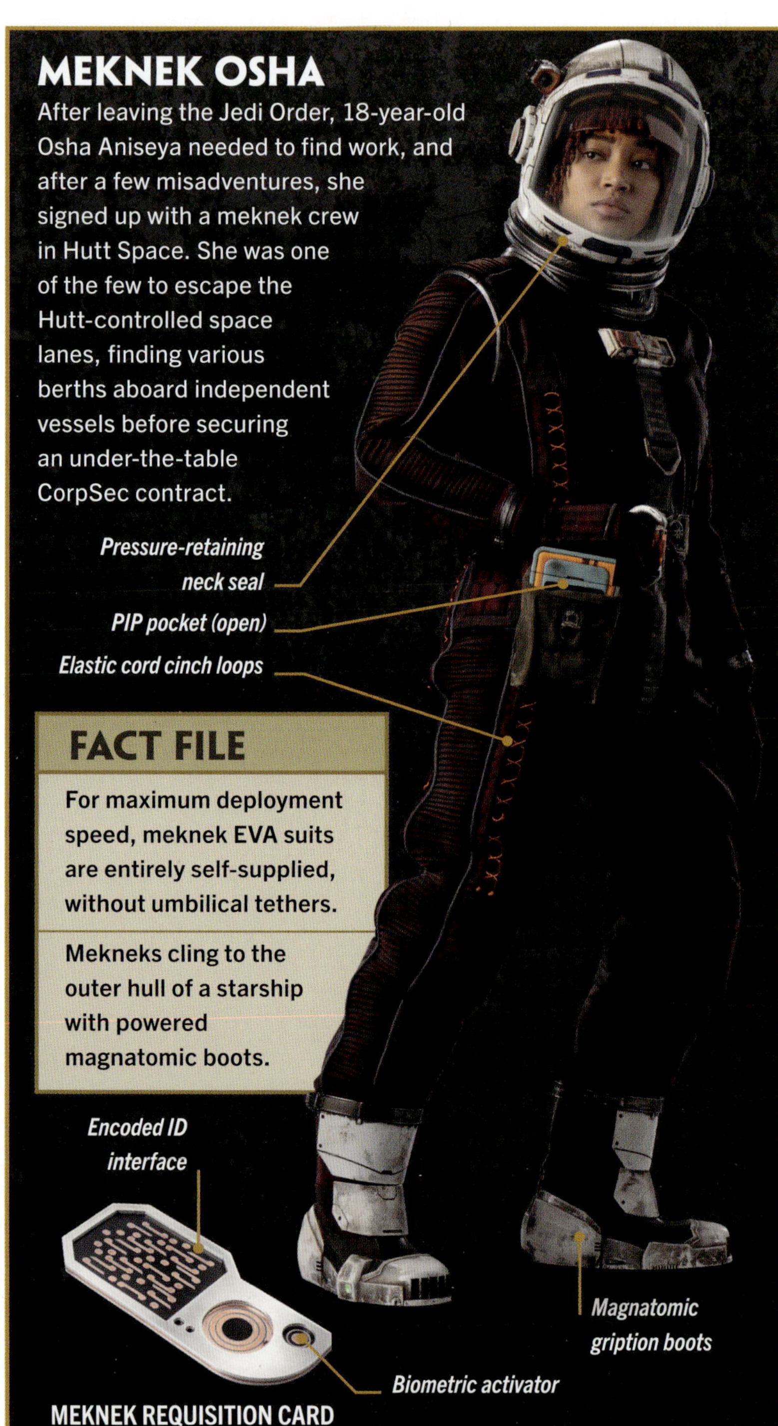

Pressure-retaining neck seal

PIP pocket (open)

Elastic cord cinch loops

FACT FILE

- For maximum deployment speed, meknek EVA suits are entirely self-supplied, without umbilical tethers.
- Mekneks cling to the outer hull of a starship with powered magnatomic boots.

Encoded ID interface

Biometric activator

Magnatomic gription boots

MEKNEK REQUISITION CARD

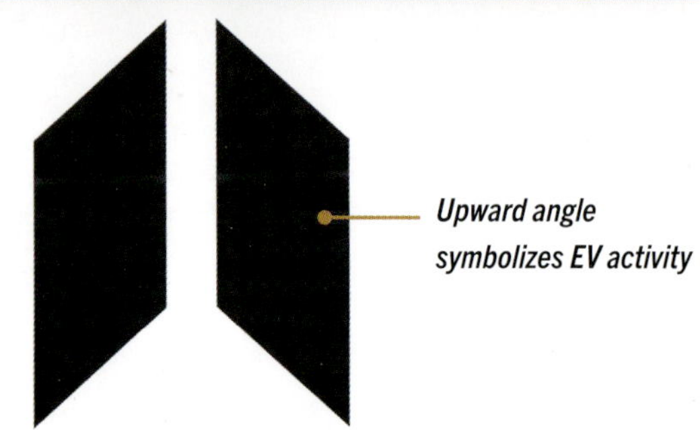

LASTING MEMORY
A rowdy night on Etti IV led to Osha and Fillik getting meknek tag tattoos; Osha has no regrets.

Upward angle symbolizes EV activity

FILLIK

Meknek work is one of the few avenues humans from Hutt Space or nearby may find to advance beyond a lower-class lifestyle. Fillik did not want his future dictated by a fickle Hutt crime lord, so he parlayed his technical skills to travel beyond the confines of the region.

Hair kept short to fit helmet

"THOSE GREASE-GRUBBERS ARE DISPOSABLE. OUR CARGO IS NOT."
CAPTAIN BLEX, ABOUT MEKNEKS

FACT FILE

Fillik has not divulged his first name, suggesting a hidden history.

The exact location of Fillik's meknek tattoo is as much a mystery as his first name.

Droid head retracted unless needed

Carousel includes custom tools

PIP DROID
Fillik has his own PIP droid, but, unlike Osha, he doesn't coddle it.

PIP unit in side-slung pocket

Multilayered sealed EVA glove

PIP unit holster

Reinforced and articulated layer

DATA FILE

SUBJECT	Fillik
HOMEWORLD	Kwenn
SPECIES	Human
AFFILIATION	Meknek
HEIGHT	1.8 m (6 ft)
AGE	26 standard years

SUITED UP
Fillik is experienced in microgravity environments, having spent much of his childhood in orbital space around Kwenn Space Station. He finds it liberating.

A/KT unisuit workwear

Electrically grounded work boots

YORD FANDAR

Jedi Yord Fandar is a man of high standards and sees the role of the Order to be an exemplar of greatness across a broad spectrum of attributes. He fully commits to continuing training to improve his already impressive abilities, and his path from Padawan to Knight was marked with awards. Yord has logged many hours as a volunteer Jedi Temple Guard and meticulously journals his exercises to track any improvements in the exacting criteria that he alone sets. He is fluent in 16 languages, including Tynnan, Shyriiwook, Sy Bisti, and even Old High Trammic. The young Jedi is only two years into knighthood; much of his knowledge is academic and not from direct experience.

Those that are closest to him take his determination with a touch of good humor, as Yord's constant striving for perfection can sometimes border on the absurd. On first glance, his overbearing confidence might be read as pride or arrogance, but it is rooted in a devotion to duty and responsibility. Yord wants to make a difference, not for himself, but for the good of the galaxy.

JEDI FINERY

Yord painstakingly maintains his appearance through the flawless presentation of his formal robes and mission apparel. He spent several years of studious duty as a youngling helping Jedi Master Robula maintain the Temple vestry, and he grew to appreciate the symbolism of color and pattern within the older Jedi traditions. Yord believes a Jedi can defuse potential conflict through an impeccable first impression.

Yord coats fabric with electrostatic fixative to repel dust

Lightsaber at the ready for quick draw

Oil treatment keeps synth-leather boots supple

JEDI VECTOR V-3

The mainstay Jedi starfighter is the Vector; variations of the ship have been in service for more than a century. The latest model is the V-3.

Powerplant chambers duct energy to thrusters and forward laser cannons

DATA FILE

MANUFACTURER	Valkeri-Kuat Consolidated Enterprises
MODEL	Vector V-3.2 Tandem
TYPE	Starfighter
DIMENSIONS	Height: 3.45 m (11 ft 4 in); Length: 14.62 m (48 ft); Width: 19.76 m (64 ft 10 in)
SPEED	100 megalight per hour; Atmospheric: 1,100 kph (683 mph)
WEAPONS	2 heavy laser cannons; 1 proton torpedo launcher
AFFILIATION	Jedi Order

TASI LOWA

While some Jedi wait years to pass on knowledge to an apprentice, Yord took on a Padawan learner soon after becoming a Knight. Tasi Lowa proves to be an exceptional pupil, living up to Yord's expectations. When not on assignment, Tasi teaches Republic civics to younglings at the Temple.

Colored Padawan sash indicates Tasi carries a green-bladed lightsaber

Encrypted datapad preloaded with mission-specific documentation

Temple robes can also serve as formal diplomatic wear

DATA FILE

SUBJECT	Tasi Lowa
HOMEWORLD	Iliabath
SPECIES	Zygerrian
AFFILIATION	Jedi Order
HEIGHT	1.6 m (5 ft 4 in)
AGE	19 standard years

INSIGHT AND MOTIVATION

Yord was a contemporary of Osha Aniseya, and though he was not privy to all the details that brought her into the Jedi Order under exceptional circumstances, he was insightful enough to read that she was haunted by them. As Yord pushed her to excel, the two settled into a friendship full of jesting barbs and playful comebacks. Osha's departure from the Order only drove Yord to push himself further.

ELECTROBINOCULARS

Yord carries holorecording electrobinoculars to gather intel on missions. The Jedi use them to study the actions of the mysterious Mae.

CLOTHES STEAMER

Yord is so particular about his appearance that he travels with a full tailoring kit, including an Ayelixe Fabrico clothes steamer to iron out any imperfections in his appearance.

DATA FILE

DATA FILE
SUBJECT Yord Fandar
HOMEWORLD Alderaan
SPECIES Human
AFFILIATION Jedi Order
HEIGHT 1.83 m (6 ft)
AGE 25 standard years

YORD'S LIGHTSABER

Yord's handcrafted lightsaber creates a vibrant yellow blade often associated with the Temple Guards of the Order, a symbol of stalwart vigilance.

FACT FILE

Yord's spiked earring is a mark of decoration given in gratitude by the High Irecha of Iridonia.

As a Padawan, Yord organized intramural sporting events among the Jedi apprentices to hone physical and mental skills.

JEDI TEMPLE

Dominating the skyline amid a crop of towers that seem flimsy in comparison is a stout ziggurat crowned by five soaring spires—the unmistakable silhouette of the Jedi Temple. Its current configuration has stood undisturbed for centuries. While its harsh face rarely changes, the interior undergoes reconfigurations and evolutions to keep up with the ever-present demands the galaxy places on the Jedi Order. Its polished halls teem with representatives from across the Republic seeking to petition the attention of the Jedi.

DATA FILE

REGION Core

SECTOR Corusca

SYSTEM Coruscant

DIAMETER 12,240 km (7,606 miles)

TERRAIN Concentric levels of city sprawl

MOONS 4

POPULATION 2,981,780,000,000* (*estimate)

CABEN JIOR
Tasked as a liaison with the influential Byne Guild of spacers, Jedi Knight Caben Jior monitors reports from far-flung travelers.

FLURRI WISS
A Jedi Knight who helps administer visitors to the Temple, Flurri Wiss is an expert on Tynnan culture and interacts with their delegation.

Mission robes for offworld travel

Seal of the late High Republic

Jedi utility belt

"CONNECT TO THE FORCE. HAVE FAITH. THINK OF DIVING INTO A GREAT OCEAN, GIVE YOURSELVES OVER TO ITS WEIGHT, ITS STILLNESS, ITS UNCERTAINTY."

MASTER SOL, INSTRUCTING YOUNGLINGS

LAYERS OF HISTORY

The deepest levels of the Temple cut down through Coruscant's urban sprawl to dark recesses below, which serve as a stratified record of the past. The Order's focus is skyward, to the future.

Embassy landing areas for offworld visitors

Central spire houses galactic communications hub

JEDI TEMPLE LOCATIONS

TACTICAL BRIEFING ROOM
Analysis of information from across the galaxy occurs in modern state-of-the-art briefing rooms that keep the Jedi Order abreast of crises.

LAUNCH BAYS
While the Temple spires house smaller launch pads, the main ziggurat has facilities for larger Jedi ships and visiting vessels.

TRAINING VERANDAH
Jedi pupils practice in airy verandas with potentially distracting views of the cityscape; maintaining focus is an exercise in itself.

DETAINMENT CELLS
Deeply ensconced in the Temple are high-tech cells where lawbreakers are held for questioning before handover to the Judiciary.

MASTER LAKSHAY
An apprentice to the renowned lightsaber virtuoso Vo'ren Faalo, Master Lakshay continues in his footsteps, instructing Jedi of all ages in time-tested techniques.

JEV EREMIA
When Jev Eremia meditates, he feels the Force as a flame, nurturing and warming when carefully tended but to be respected for its destructive potential.

XILAWA DATER
Xilawa Dater has a strong sense of life, which she demonstrates in exercises in the Temple arboreta.

Younglings wear colorless sashes

KHARI SENDO
A youngling from the Majestic Aiwha Clan, Khari Sendo shows early signs of leadership and dispute-settling potential. She encourages her fellow students to open up with their feelings.

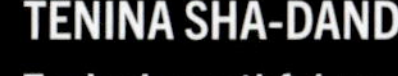

TENINA SHA-DAND
Tenina's youthful energy bypasses her shyness and manifests itself in sculptural works she produces while in meditation.

Cross-legged meditation pose

CHIPPIN JAT
A young Celantes, Chippin hatched four years ago to parents proud to deliver him to the Jedi Temple for testing and training.

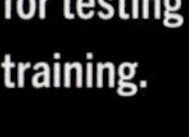

SOL

As Sol has aged into the rank of Jedi Master, he has come closer to the ideal of a compassionate yet measured mentor. Not visible upon his serene surface are the wounds required to reach this state of balance and wisdom. Also unseen is just how fragile a foundation this balance is built upon.

In his youth, Sol's confidence led to rash decisions and calamitous missteps upon his finding of Osha Aniseya as a prospective Padawan. He tried wholeheartedly to protect the young girl from the tragedies of her past, but despite his best efforts, her apprenticeship foundered. Sol has grown in the years since, showing great wisdom with his current apprentice Jecki Lon. She can see the spark of emotions in Sol as Osha returns to his life.

SOL, JEDI KNIGHT

In his younger days, Sol possessed a disarming boldness that let him confidently hold discourse and even debate with the more wizened Jedi Masters. Some in the Order were concerned that such assuredness could lead to a miscalculation when it came to challenges requiring a more delicate approach.

"THE FORCE IS POWERFUL. LIKE FIRE OR THE OCEAN, IT IS A POWER WE MUST RESPECT."
SOL

Lightsaber grip kept close to vertical to allow broad range of repositioning

Knees and hips kept flexible to rapidly adapt as needed

Back foot in firm stance for pivoting and power

Left foot forward in traditional engagement stance

Service channel and power assembly access

Grip panels for secure hold in older holsters

SOL'S LIGHTSABER

SOL, JEDI MASTER

Jedi Master Sol was in no rush to take a Padawan learner, until his discovery of Osha Aniseya's remarkable potential. The unique and tumultuous circumstances in which she was found helped make the case to train her at the advanced age of eight. Despite much promise, her path led elsewhere.

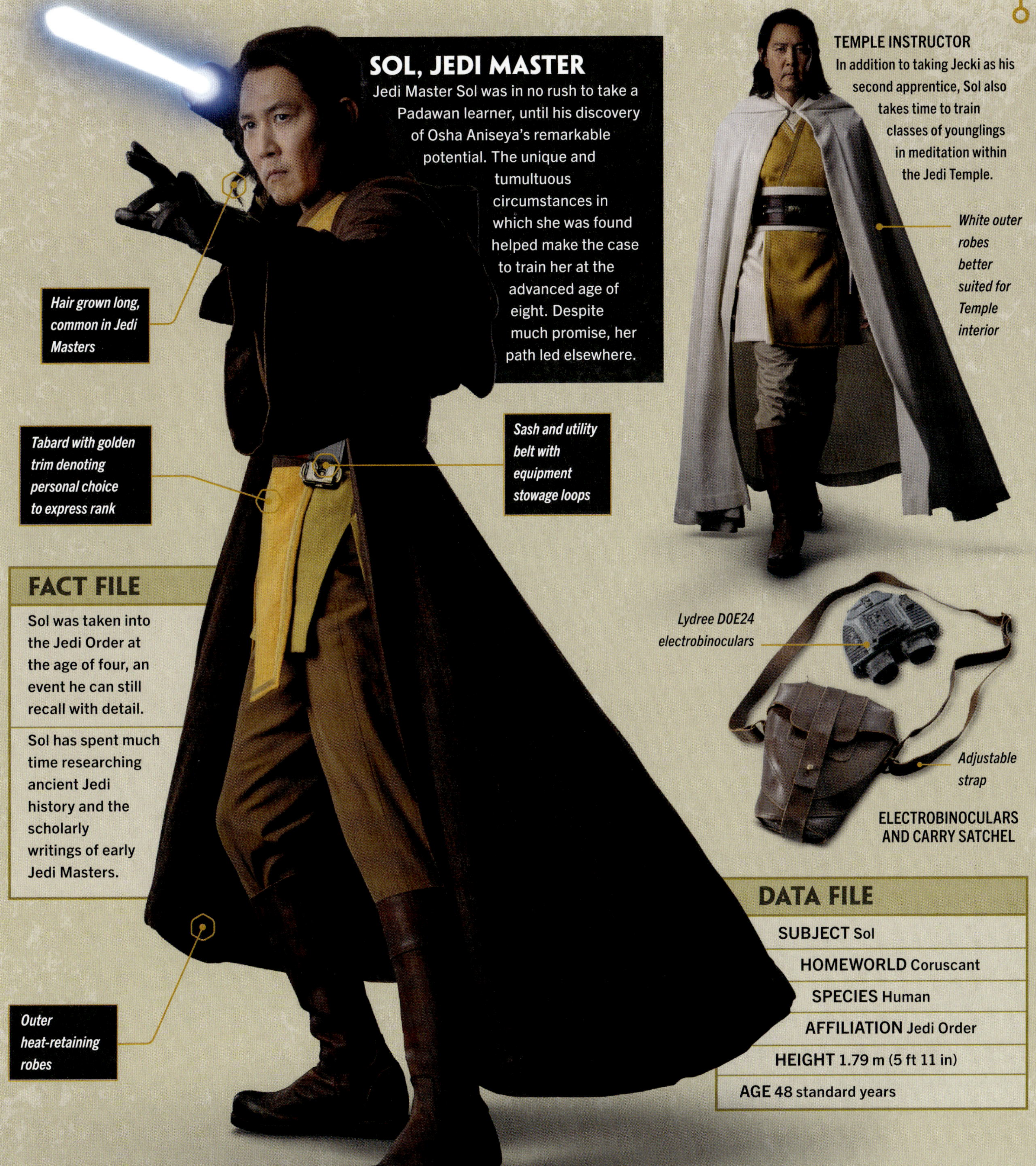

Hair grown long, common in Jedi Masters

Tabard with golden trim denoting personal choice to express rank

Sash and utility belt with equipment stowage loops

Outer heat-retaining robes

TEMPLE INSTRUCTOR

In addition to taking Jecki as his second apprentice, Sol also takes time to train classes of younglings in meditation within the Jedi Temple.

White outer robes better suited for Temple interior

Lydree D0E24 electrobinoculars

Adjustable strap

ELECTROBINOCULARS AND CARRY SATCHEL

FACT FILE

Sol was taken into the Jedi Order at the age of four, an event he can still recall with detail.

Sol has spent much time researching ancient Jedi history and the scholarly writings of early Jedi Masters.

DATA FILE

SUBJECT Sol

HOMEWORLD Coruscant

SPECIES Human

AFFILIATION Jedi Order

HEIGHT 1.79 m (5 ft 11 in)

AGE 48 standard years

JECKI LON

A studious and bright Padawan apprenticed to Master Sol, Jecki Lon is a diligent learner. She holds herself to a rigid formality when in the presence of her master, but among peers, she is more relaxed and even playful.

The relationship of master and Padawan is one of the most revered pillars of the Jedi Order, a fundamental circle of learning where information, wisdom, and traditions are passed along over a thousand generations. These pairings are typically approved—and in some cases, orchestrated—by the Jedi Council, meeting criteria that the respected body finds most beneficial for both mentor and apprentice.

As his Padawan, Jecki is rarely far from Sol's side. Though she has accompanied her master as an observer on past assignments, the mission to Carlac represents her first outing as an active partner.

THE JEDI ARTS

Dueling is largely an academic pursuit, as it is rare to find combatants who are competent enough to truly challenge a Jedi, or to wield a lightsaber with ill intent. But Jedi heritage emphasizes preparedness and finds the connection and clarity unlocked in combat readiness of benefit. The more instinctive the defensive actions are, the less potential for anger to drive them.

TEMPLE TRAINING

Jecki Lon excels in sparring classes. She welcomes the varied experiences from wielding bokken of different lengths, weights, and substances, and challenges herself by training with equipment classed for physically larger students.

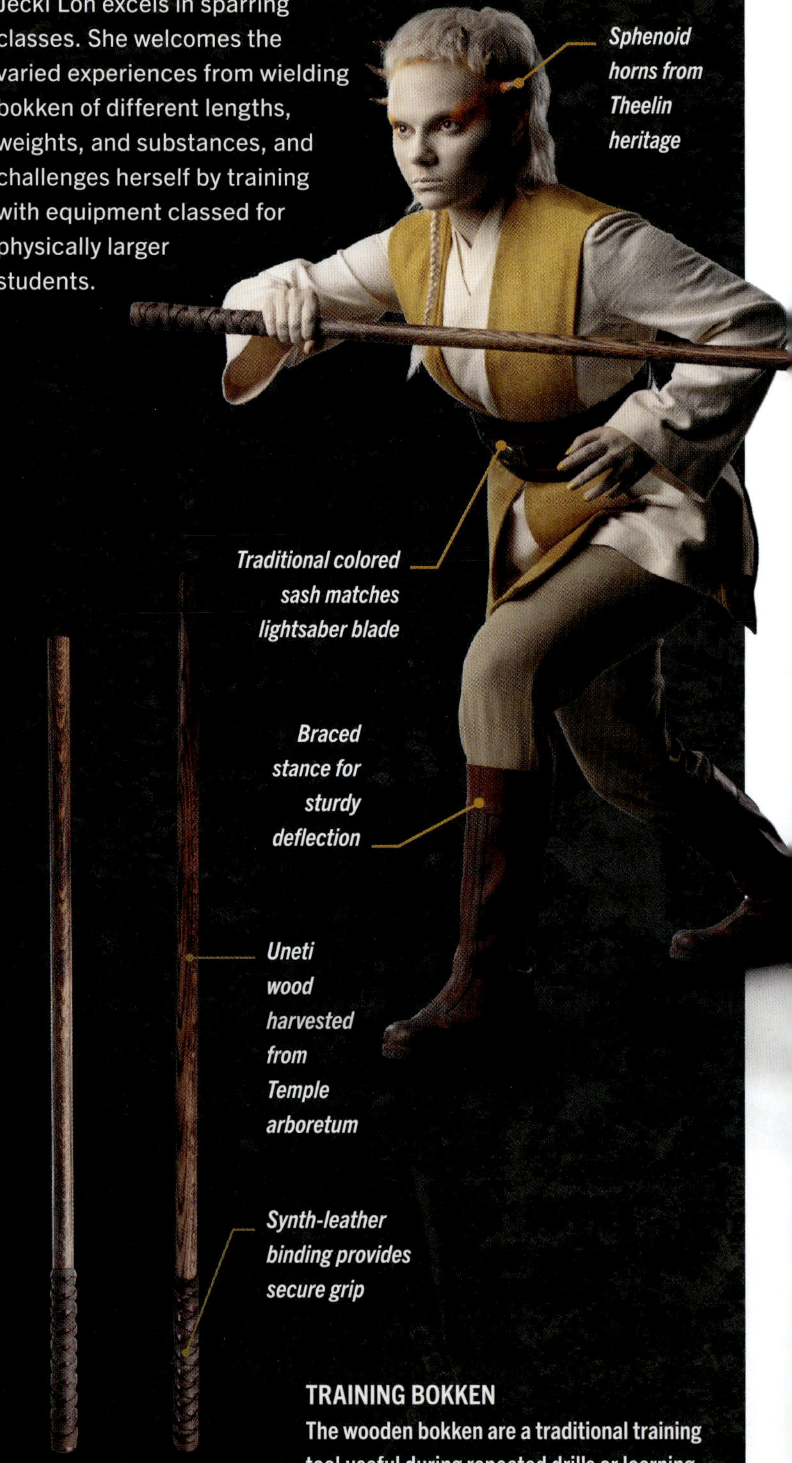

Sphenoid horns from Theelin heritage

Traditional colored sash matches lightsaber blade

Braced stance for sturdy deflection

Uneti wood harvested from Temple arboretum

Synth-leather binding provides secure grip

1-METER (40-INCH) BOKKEN

1.10-METER (43-INCH) BOKKEN

TRAINING BOKKEN

The wooden bokken are a traditional training tool useful during repeated drills or learning new forms. They are durable and safe, though they can cause blunt trauma if carelessly handled.

DRIVEN TO EXCEL

Specialized training rooms within the Jedi Temple incorporate automated systems that animate a variety of obstacle courses to physically challenge and surprise Padawan learners. Jecki Lon is known to modify these controls, testing herself at limits beyond those within safety protocols. She skirts the boundaries of recklessness, taking on risks with good humor.

FACT FILE

PADAWAN PILOT
Aside from her lightsaber skills, Jecki also focuses on her piloting ability in sims and aboard the *Polan*.

MEASURED RIVALRY
Four years separate Jecki and Yord Fandar. In part due to their close age, the pair see themselves as being like siblings.

DATA FILE

SUBJECT Jecki Lon

HOMEWORLD Coruscant

SPECIES Mixed Theelin/human heritage

AFFILIATION Jedi Order

HEIGHT 1.61 m (5 ft 3 in)

AGE 21 standard years

VERNESTRA RWOH

As a child, Vernestra Rwoh was an excellent student who leapt through the ranks of the Jedi Order at a phenomenal rate. At the age when most young Jedi were only entering apprenticeship to a master, she had already completed her trials to become a Jedi Knight. Shortly thereafter, Vernestra began teaching an apprentice of her own, herself barely older than her student.

Some may label her an overachiever—as a long-lived Mirialan with a lifespan that could reach into centuries, there seemed no need for hurry. But such observations did little justice to Vernestra's drive to excellence. This motivation propelled her into the heart of the Nihil crisis—an opportunity to prove her worth but also a taste of just how difficult the life of a Jedi could be.

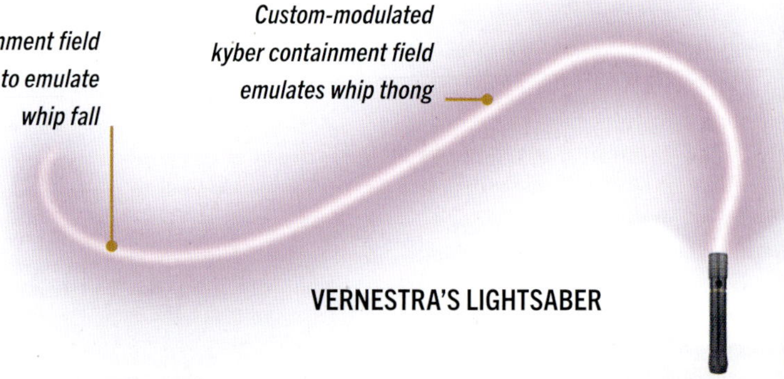

Containment field tapers to emulate whip fall

Custom-modulated kyber containment field emulates whip thong

VERNESTRA'S LIGHTSABER

JEDI DIPLOMATIC TOWER

Located near the Jedi Temple is a tower that serves as a meeting place between Jedi and Senate representatives.

MOG ADANA

Eager to be helpful to the Jedi Masters he deeply respects, Mog Adana serves in the liaison groups that connect the Jedi Order and the Galactic Senate. Mog is well aware of Vernestra Rwoh's matchless reputation, and humbly serves this model of Jedi duty. He abides by Vernestra's preference for secrecy and independent investigation.

Jedi belt has small comlink with extensive contact list tucked inside

Tabard in temple gold hues

Temple wear kept pristine for diplomatic liaisons

Immaculately polished boots

DATA FILE

SUBJECT Mog Adana
HOMEWORLD Coruscant
SPECIES Human
AFFILIATION Jedi Order
HEIGHT 1.85 m (6 ft)
AGE 26 standard years

Lacquered wood finish

Emitter guard

MOG ADANA'S LIGHTSABER

"DISCRETION IS IMPORTANT. OUR JUSTICE SWIFT. AN EXAMPLE MADE."

VERNESTRA RWOH TO SOL

CAUTIOUS MASTER

Vernestra sees enemies to the Jedi Order behind the practiced smiles and salutary handshakes of supposed allies in the Senate, where there is a growing current of political hostility. Jedi methods are undergoing scrutiny by those eager to impose procedure on an independent arm of the Judiciary.

Hooded sleeveless robe

FACT FILE

In her teens, the precocious Vernestra fashioned a customized lightsaber with a light-whip mode, a weapon she still carries.

During hyperspace journeys, Vernestra feels unsettled and will occasionally experience visions, especially if meditating.

Gold-trimmed temple dress with compression sleeves

Heavy woven material with green and gold woolen fibers

DRESSED WITH PURPOSE
Having to regularly interface with non-Jedi delegates, Vernestra Rwoh dresses in diplomatic robes when required.

DATA FILE

SUBJECT	Vernestra Rwoh
HOMEWORLD	Coruscant
SPECIES	Mirialan
AFFILIATION	Jedi Order
HEIGHT	1.75 m (5 ft 9 in)

Robes conceal utility belt

Textured white Ghor silk dress

Heavy formal robe with box pleat back

Off-white silhouette with loose drape

PALWICK PRISON SHIP

To take suspect Osha Aniseya back to Coruscant, the Jedi enlist the assistance of a nearby prison transport vessel, the *Palwick*. The Corporate Sector (CorpSec) has its own independent law enforcement arm; in cases that fall under Jedi jurisdiction, the Order can commandeer resources such as this prison ship, when necessary. This prevents the need for the Jedi to have a standing captivity fleet.

Hyperdrive engine connected to power-hub cradle

Engineering core and reactor bulb

Long-range hyperradio antenna

Reinforced hyperdrive support pylon

DATA FILE

MANUFACTURER Kazellan Corporation

MODEL DTE-CSA-17 Calaboose

TYPE Long-range prisoner transport vessel

DIMENSIONS Height: 31.65 m (103 ft 10 in); Length: 125.94 m (413 ft); Width: 81.65 m (267 ft 10 in)

SPEED 75 megalight per hour; Atmospheric: 850 kph (528 mph)

WEAPONS None

AFFILIATION Corporate Sector Authority (CSA)

Variable geometry droids serve as pilots for the prison transport and are able to convert into seats for organic crew.

OUTSOURCED JUSTICE

The long arm of the Republic law does not stretch to the Corporate Sector, so the Republic judicial branch has crafted complex extradition treaties with the governing Corporate Sector Authority to ensure its domain doesn't become a haven for criminals fleeing Republic space. Repatriation of fugitives by CSA vessels incurs hefty bill-back fees from CorpSec, which may be collected from fines levied on the prisoners.

"WE HAVE A SUSPECT IN CUSTODY. AN OLD PADAWAN OF YOURS: OSHA ANISEYA. I SEE I HAVE UNDERESTIMATED YOUR ATTACHMENT TO HER."

VERNESTRA RWOH TO MASTER SOL

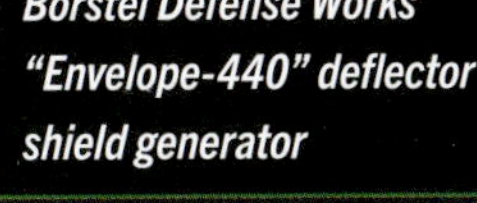

Forward port escape pod

Kazellan K-DT17c sublight engines

DYBBUK SILENCER

A dybbuk silencer is a parasitic life-form modified by Chiewab Pharmaceuticals from an atmospheric glider native to Dybrin 12. The creature feeds off the host's neural energy while transmitting euphoric alpha waves. Some subjects report terrifying nightmares during dybbuk sleep, a claim Chiewab researchers strongly deny. Study of the process is prohibited as it is a trade secret.

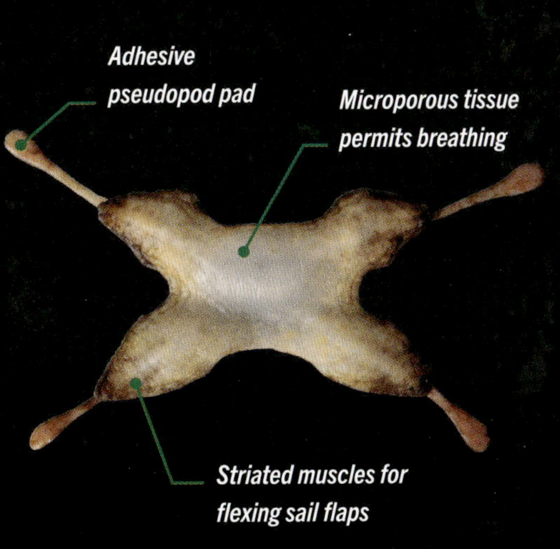

F0-4 WARDEN DROID

To prevent the possibility of bribes or coercion from the imprisoned, the Corporate Sector Authority predominantly employs automated personnel among its prison guard staff. A single Ulban Arms F0-4 warden droid keeps watch over the *Palwick*'s cells. Minimizing collateral damage means the droid lacks any ranged weaponry, but it does carry an energized baton.

PRISON BREAK

Osha Aniseya is not alone aboard the *Palwick*, as the ship carries several cells full of Corporate Sector criminals due for Detention Task Force processing. They are impressed with the rumor that Osha killed a Jedi—an unheard-of act among this particular level of lowlifes. Recognizing that a purported "Jedi Killer" would be a great asset to their retinue, the scheming criminals attempt to recruit Osha into their escape plans, but Osha has more common sense than they do.

The plan is foolhardy. Using a hybroid inmate's contraband cybernetics as a way to exploit a security flaw in the droid crew, the escapists cause the *Palwick* to drop violently from hyperspace. Emergency protocols in the navicomputer decant the ship in a star system rather than strand it in deep space, but that well-intentioned effort serves only to jeopardize the ship even further. The *Palwick* collides violently with a satellite in the Carlac belt and begins to make an unscheduled planetfall.

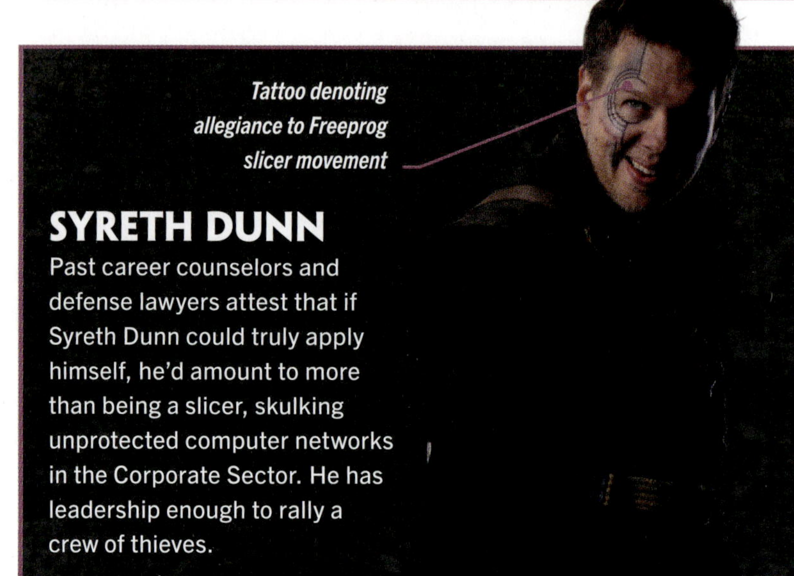

Tattoo denoting allegiance to Freeprog slicer movement

SYRETH DUNN

Past career counselors and defense lawyers attest that if Syreth Dunn could truly apply himself, he'd amount to more than being a slicer, skulking unprotected computer networks in the Corporate Sector. He has leadership enough to rally a crew of thieves.

Coiled head tentacle ready to strike

TOR BEZ'LIN

An amphibious Shorwilt, Tor Bez'lin is a skilled security expert, versed in programming and electronic lock-breaking. He also has a more brute force methodology he keeps secret until needed. His epicranial muscle is a strong, fibrous tentacle that he can propel with great speed and impact.

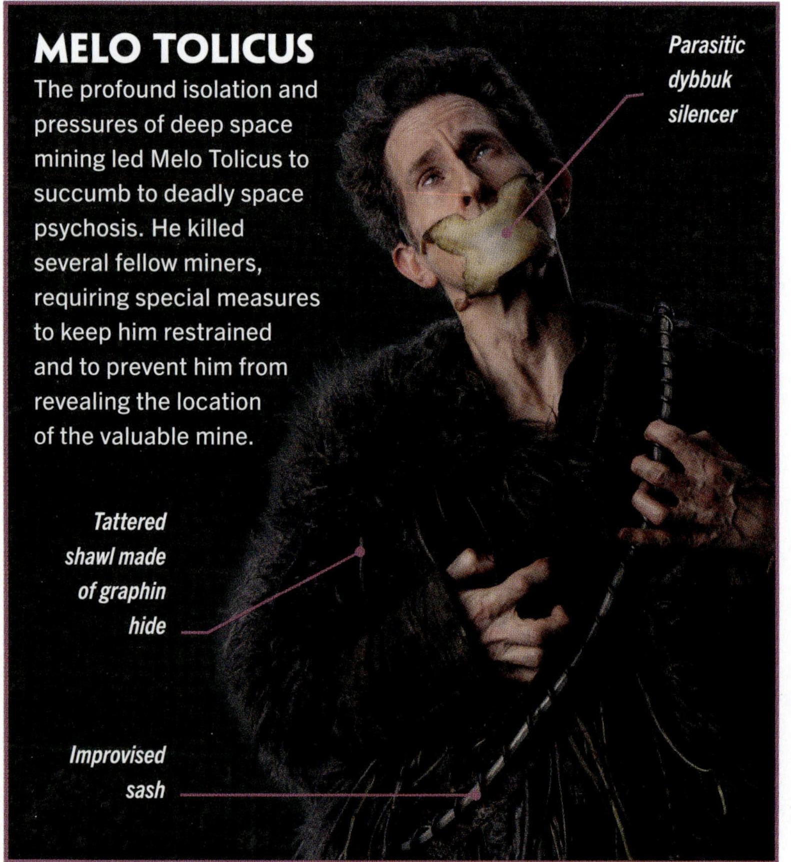

MELO TOLICUS

The profound isolation and pressures of deep space mining led Melo Tolicus to succumb to deadly space psychosis. He killed several fellow miners, requiring special measures to keep him restrained and to prevent him from revealing the location of the valuable mine.

Parasitic dybbuk silencer

Tattered shawl made of graphin hide

Improvised sash

ZARD ZELL

A Mimbanese expatriate whose keratin scutes have faded in color, Zard Zell was the least technically inclined of Dunn's crew, and he worked primarily as a getaway pilot and mechanic. Zell did not get a chance to flex his skills before the CSA Corpos impounded his speeder.

Tough reptilian hide

Insulated driving gloves

ORLUT

Cyborged optic nerve fortification lets Orlut see better than her natural Lyrobru eyes would ordinarily allow. Orlut owes Dunn credits for software upgrades that keep her in his employ.

Pockets concealed inside sash once held lockpicking tools

Hidden dagger-sheath now emptied

COLEE QUILLO

Syreth Dunn's buyer, Colee Quillo, had the misfortune of being in the wrong place at the wrong time. He had hired Dunn's services to wipe his name from the CSA ledger in order to clear an enormous debt.

Unkempt appearance from life on the run

Hidden money belt now bereft of CSA vouchers

ROTT MERCER

The secret weapon behind Dunn's slicer success is his silent partner, Rott Mercer. Extensive mod implants give Rott enhanced slicing abilities, letting him wirelessly deploy Dunn's programs into remote computer systems. Syreth also develops code to entertain Mercer's butchered mind, adding an addictive dependency to their unscrupulous relationship.

Eyes replaced by EM scanners

Vocoder and transmitter unit

Secure data cache hidden in gallbladder

Grounding bracelets to control static electricity

"SHIP'S PILOTED BY DROIDS. WE'RE GONNA TAKE 'EM OUT AND USE THE ESCAPE PODS."

SYRETH DUNN

POLAN GX-8

A reliable workhorse of a Jedi vessel, the *Polan* (designation GX-8) has been in operation for nearly 50 standard years. It is a modified Polan-717 transport manufactured by the Lantillian Shipwrights, optimized for versatility with modular internal cabin units that allow it to serve on everyday and long-distance missions. Though not particularly suited for combat, under the control of skilled pilots, the *Polan* is an intimidating foe in space battles.

Lantillian Shipwrights SRD-150c reaction drive engine

Triple laminate hull with ablative outer layer

Communications systems transmission plane

ANALYSIS SUITE
The *Polan* is intended to be a research and investigation vessel and is fitted with a sophisticated suite of sensors.

Compressed coaxium delivery capillaries (internal)

Coaxium cooling ports

Supraluminal vector guides

Astrogational sensor panel

FLIGHT DECK STATIONS
Though optimum performance requires a minimum crew of four, a single pilot could conceivably operate the *Polan* if needed.

HYPERDRIVE CRADLE
Hyperdrive miniaturization continues to be a field of innovation; long-range journeys require external engines and fuel systems to ensure safe and reliable transit across many light-years. The cradle cools and recharges in orbit while a ship makes planetfall.

Primary laser cannon power conduit trunk

Reinforced flight deck cabin module

Astronics and sensor bay

Ramscoop intake

INTERIOR TUNNELS

The *Polan* interior is efficiently allocated and delineated to pack a variety of chambers within its hull. The common area has clusters of bunks and meeting spaces, as well as a tech station and a medical bay. The upper deck includes the cockpit and a training area for Jedi to practice sparring techniques. Lower cargo bays carry camper units and speeder bikes. The aft section includes engineering crawlways and the Finchdart escape craft.

"CORUSCANT 51-12 TO *POLAN* GX-8. YOU ARE CLEAR FOR TRANSMISSION."

MOG ADANA

OPERATIONAL HISTORY

Ships, like most Jedi technology outside of lightsabers, do not have any specific owners, so the *Polan* has had a variety of pilots in its decades of service. Master Indara piloted it 16 years earlier on a fateful mission to Brendok, and thus Sol has an appreciation of the ship's performance and reliability. Sol has Jecki pilot the ship to Carlac and Olega.

DATA FILE

MANUFACTURER Lantillian Shipwrights

MODEL Polan-717

TYPE Jedi transport

DIMENSIONS (with hyperdrive attached)
Height: 20.45 m (67 ft 1 in);
Length: 78.56 m (257 ft 8 in);
Width: 58.14 m (190 ft 9 in) /
(without hyperdrive)
Height: 16.75 m (55 ft);
Length: 58.12 m (190 ft 7 in);
Width: 31.82 m (104 ft 4 in)

SPEED 90 megalight per hour;
Atmospheric: 1,050 kph (652 mph)

WEAPONS 2 forward laser cannons;
2 light blaster cannons; 1 ordnance launcher

AFFILIATION Jedi Order

CRASH ON CARLAC

The glitched hyperspace reversion throws the *Palwick* far off the Hydian Way. In an effort to compensate, the ship's scrambled navicomputer latches onto the Entralla Route before finally spitting the ship out in the Carlac system where it decelerates to sublight speed. Spinning out of control after an asteroid collision, the *Palwick* crashes to a skidding halt in the northern mountains of planet Carlac. Osha Aniseya straps herself in securely enough that she survives, albeit bruised and shaken.

"THE REPUBLIC DISPATCHED PROBE DROIDS TO SURVEY THE WRECKAGE."
VERNESTRA RWOH TO MASTER SOL

Fold mountain outcropping from ancient thrust tectonics

Arch formed from expanding frozen water and wind erosion

A WORLD FAR FROM NOTICE
Carlac is in the Prefsbelt sector, a little remarked upon expanse in the Outer Rim reputed to be the source of the mynock.

DATA FILE

REGION Outer Rim

SECTOR Prefsbelt

SYSTEM Carlac

DIAMETER 9,494 km (5,899 miles)

TERRAIN Frigid mountain chains; cold blue-sand deserts

MOONS None, but there is a loose asteroidal ring

POPULATION Less than 10,000

VISIONS OF FIRE

As Osha recovers from the crash, she is struck by strange visions of a very familiar young girl—her twin sister, Mae. The girl appears as Osha last saw her years earlier, when a devastating fire consumed their home. The nightmarish apparition startles Osha awake.

REUNION

The crew of the *Polan* finds the wreckage of the *Palwick* and tracks Osha from the shattered wreck to nearby caves. It is a reunion for Osha, who hasn't seen her former master, Sol, in years. She insists on her innocence, and Sol believes her.

CARLAC

A planet with sparse habitations in the southern latitudes, Carlac is a frozen world of mountainous landscapes. A Yarkora colony has settled in the blue equatorial deserts, while Ming Po monks are raising monasteries further north. This is all far away from the Piteous Ranges, a subpolar mountain chain devoid of even primitive lichens.

Snow intermixed with blue dust particles swept from lower latitudes

Molasse rock made from primeval marine deposits

CHAPTER 2

THE SECOND TARGET

Secured within an outpost temple on Olega, Mae Aniseya's next target is Jedi Master Torbin. As he meditates on past failures, she enters the temple to carry out her dark assignment but finds an impenetrable barrier protecting Torbin. Mae switches tactics, trading the edge of a blade for the extract of bunta poison as her weapon, a move that will satisfy her need for vengeance if not the requirements of her master.

OLEGA

Millennia ago, when Olega was at the outer edge of Republic space, its island capital was a bulwarked fortress filled with Jedi guardians protecting the frontier from outlying threats. Shifting fortunes and further galactic expansion left that role in the distant past. Olega City still has formidable walls and a modest, downsized Jedi temple, but it is not at the precipice of conflict. Instead, the city is now a hive of active marketplaces, attracting travelers with bespoke and artisanal wares.

DATA FILE
REGION Mid Rim
SECTOR Esuian
SYSTEM Olega
DIAMETER 12,104 km (7,521 miles)
TERRAIN Oceans and island chains
MOONS 3
POPULATION 265.4 million

GUTHAN ARCHI

Guthan Archi turns his inside knowledge of Olega City into credits by serving as a guide, delivery boy, and messenger. Since his face is known to the local Jedi, he does not venture into pickpocketing. However, he is not above serving as lookout or decoy while someone else does.

Loose vest to shed if caught

Tunic with hidden pockets for coins

STREET VENDORS

SCRAP VENDOR
Tu-Shaz trawls the tidal basins for metallic and plastic refuse, cleans it up, and sells it in the street market.

FLATBREAD BAKER
The scents from Gwira Bolani's oven attract customers eager for her unleavened and conveniently portable specialties with exotic toppings.

METALSMITH
Melting down and reforging scrap and raw materials, Troha Sor (right) and his apprentice Rovo craft metal goods, both decorative and practical.

GREENGROCER
Otta Chorrall has a cavern garden outside the Olega City walls where she cultivates a variety of nutritious fruits and vegetables.

I-ZELLAM

With his keen sensory organs clustered around his trunk, ears, and horns, I-Zellam is impeccably qualified to detect expert craftwork in handmade goods.

THAKIRA TATARA

Spiritual horticulturists Thakira Tatara and her sister Kiraya travel from the Southern Isles to Olega City with exotic seeds and sprigs to sell.

KIRAYA TATARA

While her sister Thakira concentrates on nutritive plants, Kiraya Tatara focuses on medicinal growing. She supplies the local apothecary and healing houses with balms and oils harvested from her greenhouse.

Handloomed seed satchel

MARKET KIDS

The youngest members of an impoverished family are often the ones earning the most through odd jobs and handouts.

Tartan pattern indicates Godis Ulani's home neighborhood

ASALA SURO

Though the reclusive Umbarans favor more overcast worlds, Asala Suro and her wife, Cosa Simo, have ventured into the walled city on personal business.

Bundled clothing protects light-sensitive skin

COSA SIMO

Cosa Simo is tracing her ancestry with the help of Asala, an archivist. Cosa has found a familial line dating back more than 3,000 years to Olega. She hopes to access the ancient records kept in the Jedi temple.

Travel shadowcloak

OLEGA JEDI TEMPLE

The High Republic era is marked by a more decentralized Jedi Order, with satellite outposts scattered far from the main Jedi Temple on Coruscant. Many date back to an earlier time when lengthy hyperspace journeys were not as reliable. Jedi would head to outlying systems, providing protection to distant Republic worlds that denoted the outward frontier.

Like the one on Olega, many outpost temples are old, drafty, and spartan. The foundation stones of the Olega building are at least 17,000 years old, though its current configuration is younger than a millennium. Similar to other sanctuaries, the temple on Olega is built at a place where a deep Force vision occurred. In this case, it was a visiting Jedi Master, Olega-Dann, who felt compelled to stay and bring the Republic to an otherwise uninhabited but vibrant world. The planet still bears a fragment of this master's name, but few locals know this aspect of their own history. The Jedi outpost is seen as an old fixture, and its Jedi as helpful neighbors.

The humble entrance barely hints at the ancient and sacred subterranean temple within.

OD KEDER

A Padawan fast approaching his time to undergo the Jedi Trials, Od Keder is well known among the Olegans that border the temple. They have seen him grow up in the neighborhood and consider him one of their own.

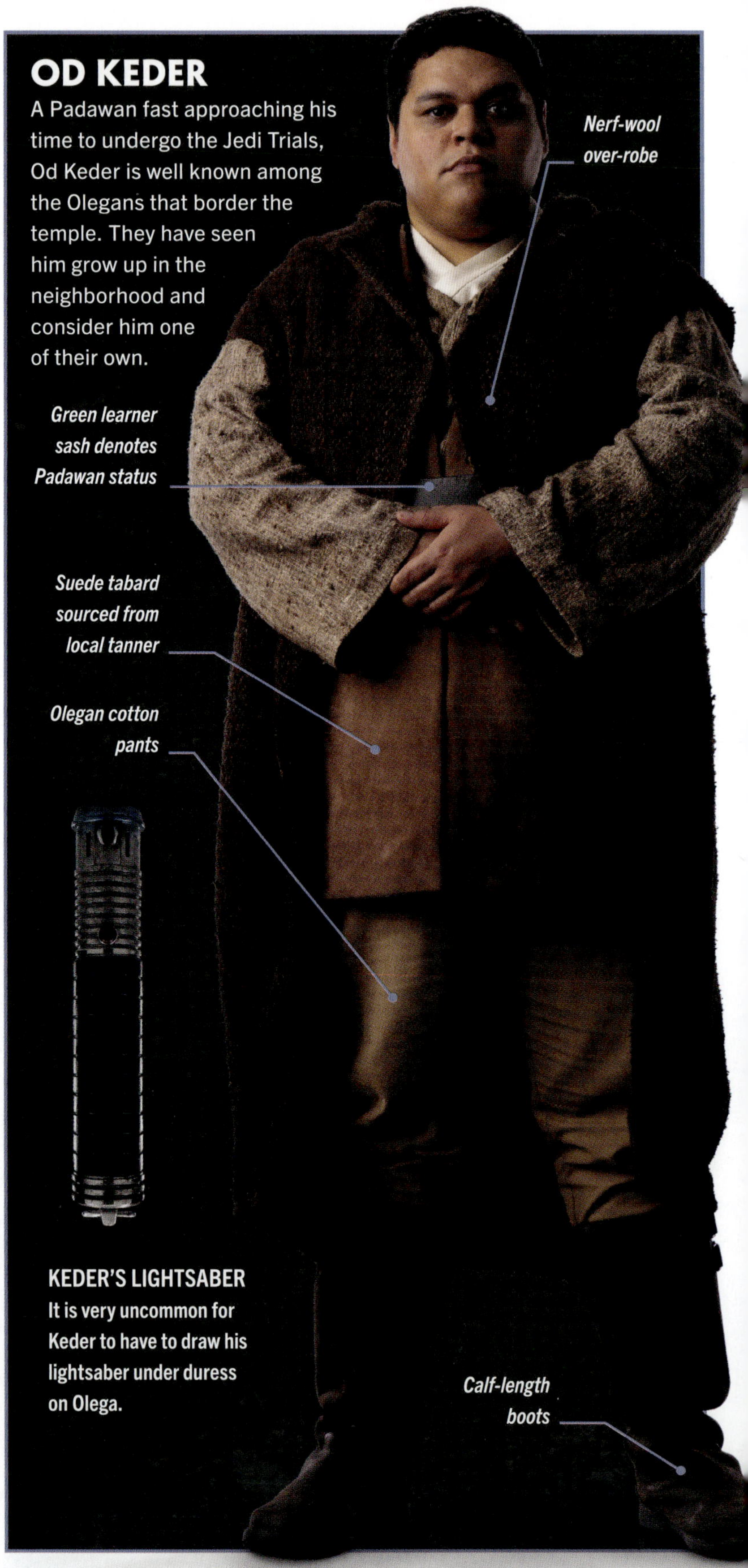

Nerf-wool over-robe

Green learner sash denotes Padawan status

Suede tabard sourced from local tanner

Olegan cotton pants

Calf-length boots

KEDER'S LIGHTSABER

It is very uncommon for Keder to have to draw his lightsaber under duress on Olega.

"WELCOME TO OLEGA. WE DIDN'T THINK CORUSCANT WOULD BE INTERESTED IN OUR LITTLE BREAK-IN."

CORD TAUNUS TO MASTER SOL

GATEKEEPER DROID

Outside the open hours when visitors can freely petition the temple, the closed doors are monitored by a tireless TT-8L gatekeeper droid. A misloaded program update has given it a surly personality. Unlike many similar models, TT-8L-OT has binocular vision, with two spheroid photoreceptors scrutinizing the world around it.

CORD TAUNUS

The Steward of Olega, Jedi Master Cord Taunus administers the local temple. Among his duties is the monitoring of Master Torbin, who has spent a decade in self-imposed isolation and deep meditation. That anyone would find Torbin a threat is unthinkable to Taunus, and he is surprised by Master Sol's visit.

Sleeveless quilted tabard

Lightsaber affixed using hilt-ring

Hilt-ring becoming increasingly common

CORD TAUNUS' LIGHTSABER
Cord Taunus has had this lightsaber since his apprenticeship, and it emits a brilliant blue blade.

Synth-leather boots

MASTER TORBIN

Sequestered in a private chamber within the Olega Jedi temple is Master Torbin, who has not spoken to anyone in years. He sits in the deepest meditation, with the intent of losing his conscious self in the currents of the Force. Torbin achieves this trance-like state to expunge past traumas from his conscience. Although he seems tranquil, this surface appearance is just a mask. Unlike others who have undergone similar meditations, Torbin exudes a turbulence in the Force that manifests itself in an unbreakable barrier.

Mae's attempts to strike at Torbin are deflected by this barrier. The impenetrable shield is a unique side effect of Torbin's Barash Vow, involuntarily erected to protect him while he probes the healing fathoms of the Force in a vain search for self-forgiveness. Mae later adopts a different tactic, aided by Qimir—targeting Torbin's need for absolution.

Mae simply places a vial of bunta poison before Torbin, offering him rest from his turmoil. Lowering to the ground, he awakens from his meditative state, aware of his surroundings and having heard her offer. With a final request for forgiveness, Torbin willingly ingests the toxin.

THE BARASH VOW

Named for a Jedi of centuries past, the Barash Vow is an extreme act of repentance committed by a Jedi who has transgressed beyond the Code. In principle, it is an inward meditation that prohibits overt use of enhanced Force abilities, a narrowing of focus to the material world. In practice, its motivations and effects can vary as they are determined by intensely personal decisions undertaken by a Jedi. Torbin's particular manifestation of the Barash Vow is sculpted by his encounter on Brendok.

TIMELINE

Age 3	Identified as having Force potential by a Jedi seeker, Torbin is given to the Order by impoverished parents living on Bonadan.
Age 16	Torbin becomes apprenticed to Master Indara.
Age 25	Accompanies Indara on a mission to Brendok. After nearly two months of exploration, they uncover a coven of Force witches. This leads to a tragic confrontation in which Torbin is injured.
Age 26	Passes his trials, achieving the rank of Jedi Knight.
Age 31	After years of studious devotion, Torbin attains the rank of master, and voyages to Olega. There, he takes the Barash Vow.
Age 41	Found dead on Olega, the second victim of Mae Aniseya.

Faded temple robes worn for a decade

Featureless obi sash; Torbin has no need for a utility belt

TORBIN REBALANCED

It is with no small sense of irony that the restless Padawan eager to keep moving spent the last decade of his life isolated in immobile meditation.

RESTLESS YOUTH

In his youth, Torbin possessed an impulse to stay ever-mobile. His aspirations to knighthood were colored by a drive to make a difference, to do something meaningful and impactful. He chafed under routine, especially methodical procedures where patience and repetition were demanded. Master Indara's approach to instruction was not to lecture but steer him along paths where he could seek answers and balance himself.

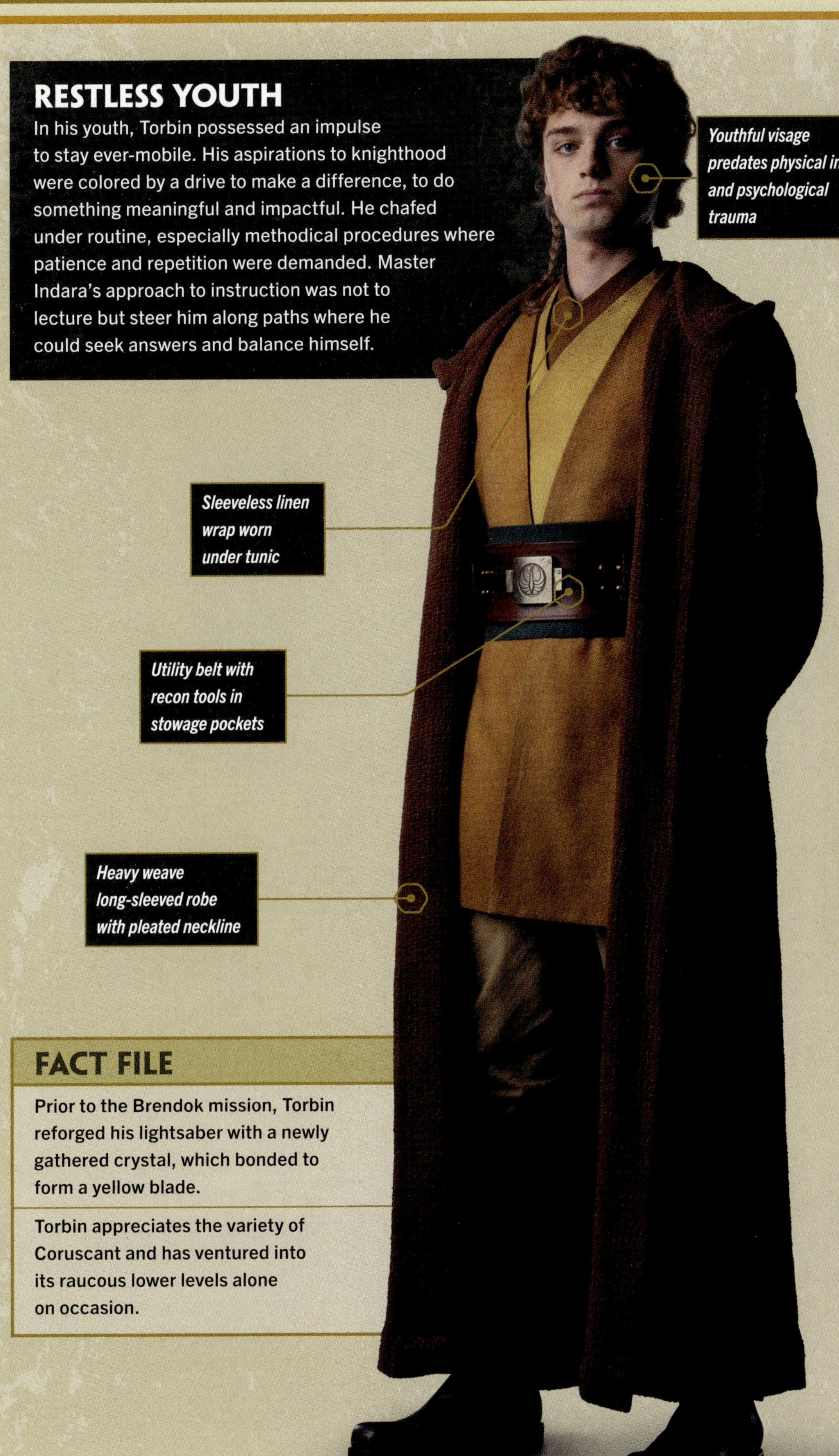

Youthful visage predates physical injury and psychological trauma

Sleeveless linen wrap worn under tunic

Utility belt with recon tools in stowage pockets

Heavy weave long-sleeved robe with pleated neckline

"I OFFER YOU A CHOICE. EITHER CONFESS YOUR CRIME TO THE JEDI COUNCIL, OR GET THE ABSOLUTION YOU SEEK RIGHT HERE, RIGHT NOW. FROM ME."

MAE ANISEYA TO MASTER TORBIN

LIGHTSABER EVOLUTION

As a Padawan, Torbin handled his lightsaber with a flourish in a defense style that emphasized an ever-moving blade, carving wide deflecting arcs around him and those behind his protection. Torbin's approach became more tempered with precision as he aged. Upon taking the Barash Vow, he relinquished his latest weapon to the Olega temple stewards.

FACT FILE

Prior to the Brendok mission, Torbin reforged his lightsaber with a newly gathered crystal, which bonded to form a yellow blade.

Torbin appreciates the variety of Coruscant and has ventured into its raucous lower levels alone on occasion.

DATA FILE

SUBJECT Master Torbin

HOMEWORLD Bonadan

SPECIES Human

AFFILIATION Jedi Order

HEIGHT 1.8 m (6 ft)

AGE 41 standard years

QIMIR

Shambling from place to place with a disarming uncertainty and carelessness, Qimir is easy to underestimate. He divulges very little about his past and appears to have no designs on the future, just living in a reckless present while trying to avoid scrutiny. The lack of responsibility is an illusion crafted with care. It draws attention away from the fact that he is in service to Mae Aniseya and their unseen master.

Qimir's latest ruse is posing as an apothecary on Olega. The real store owner has disappeared, and, if queried about it, Qimir rattles off a vague story about an extended trip to visit family. Though the apothecary role seems improvised and driven by the store's proximity to the local Jedi temple, Qimir demonstrates skill in chemistry and pharmaceuticals, indicating a deeper well of knowledge than his flippant attitude would suggest.

HYDRATING SECRETIONS
Inside a custom tank is a rare nori-inkal from Boothi IV; its fins secrete an oily serum that revitalizes aged skin and eliminates wrinkles.

A NEW APOTHECARY IN TOWN

Catherio Para opened his apothecary store more than 30 years ago and is regarded as an eccentric among the locals. He often takes extended trips to gather exotic supplies, so his absence is not remarked upon, although his "substitute"—Qimir—is a stranger on Olega.

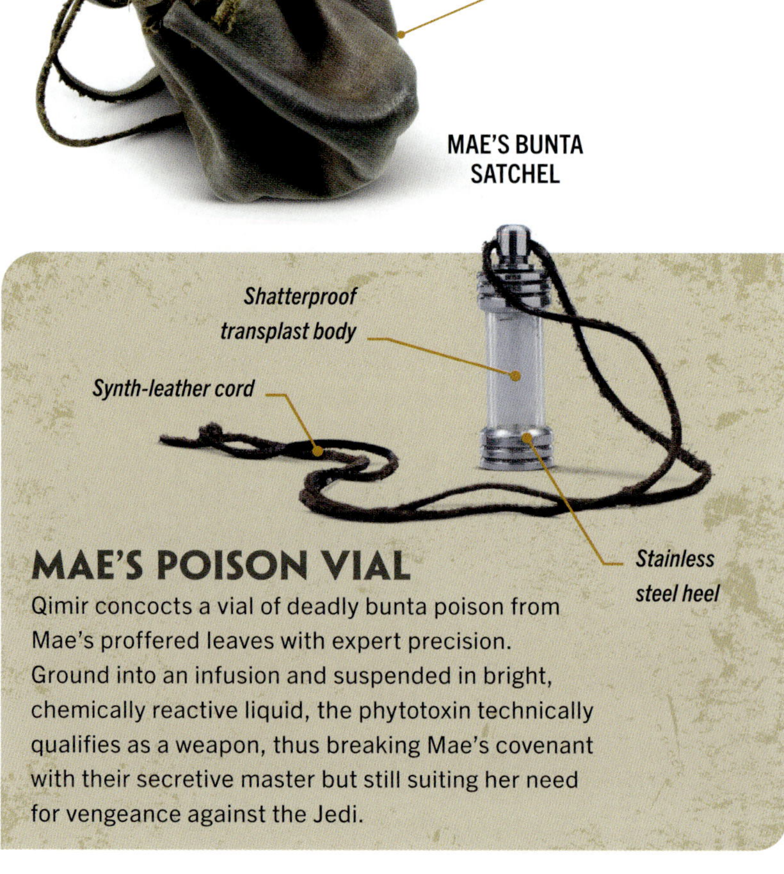

MAE'S POISON VIAL

Qimir concocts a vial of deadly bunta poison from Mae's proffered leaves with expert precision. Ground into an infusion and suspended in bright, chemically reactive liquid, the phytotoxin technically qualifies as a weapon, thus breaking Mae's covenant with their secretive master but still suiting her need for vengeance against the Jedi.

TRICKSTER DRIFTER

Qimir withdraws from conflict if possible and avoids the attention of authorities such as the vigilant Jedi Knights. If cornered, he'll attempt to talk his way out of trouble, peppering his speech with enough uncertainty that he'll sound uninformed and in way over his head. It's a time-honed strategy that has yet to fail him, and his greatest resource is the extent that those in power misjudge him.

Double-walled bottle

INSULATED HIP FLASK

Long, loose collar that can serve as a face covering

20x acrylic optical lens with polarized coating

APOTHECARY GOGGLES

Assisting Qimir in the concoction of potions both useful and recreational are a set of antiquated magni-goggles left in the store by the original owner. Their variable lenses allow close examination of medicinal ingredients.

Short-sleeve shirt with drawstring fasteners

Pockets hidden within lining

"I DO REALLY BELIEVE THAT, THOUGH: EVERYONE HAS A WEAKNESS."

QIMIR TO MAE ANISEYA

Olegan wood handle

325-ml (11-fl oz) capacity

MUG OF CARNELIAN ALE

A skilled craft brewer, Qimir samples local beers on his many travels.

FACT FILE

Qimir has spent some time gunrunning in Hutt Space—yet another detail of his life he keeps under wraps.

A close examination of Qimir's bumbling clumsiness reveals it to be an affectation.

DATA FILE

SUBJECT Qimir

HOMEWORLD Unknown

SPECIES Human

AFFILIATION None

HEIGHT 1.82 m (6 ft)

AGE Unknown

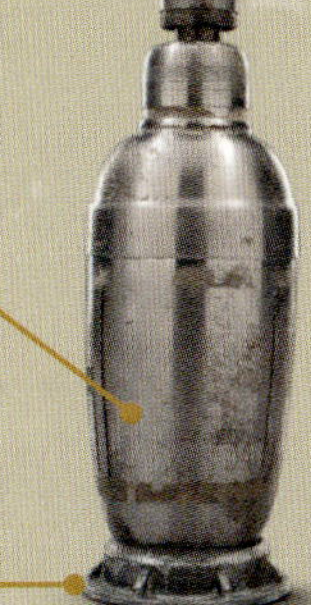

Adjustable gauge strainer dam (internal)

Weighted base

KINETIC BLENDER

ESCAPE FROM OLEGA

A break in the case surfaces when Osha poses as Mae and enters the apothecary to interact with Qimir, who makes a veiled reference to an elusive master. Using Master Sol as bait, the Jedi draws out Mae, but the young assassin proves to be a slippery quarry. She escapes the trap in a stolen landspeeder but makes eye contact with Osha for the first time in 16 years.

PDX-28 STUN BLASTER
Implemented by Vernestra Rwoh, stun blasters are a nonstandard part of the Jedi gear used when apprehension missions warrant them. Neural-disrupting energy patterns are enhanced by pulsed kinetic waves.

Assembly point for custom stun barrel attachment

Kinetic wave guide emitters

LUNTOBETHA

Her face concealed by an old Bando Gora rebreather mask, Luntobetha's appearance looks more threatening than helpful, but the locals know her well. She is a dyer working from a streetside stall in Olega City.

Repurposed and repainted rebreather mask protects from caustic dye fumes

Atmo-scanner and filter rebalancer

Concealed money belt

Cinch straps can pull jacket tight

ANBERT DREGIL

A burly Kogini, Anbert Dregil is a scrap merchant, hired hauler, stevedore, and collector of camera equipment, who is commonly known around town by nicknames like "Long Arms" and "Ol' Gundark."

Eyes can see in the ultraviolet end of the spectrum

NOSLI TILBRUK

An aging Abednedo, Nosli Tilbruk is an unlicensed courier whose fading memory for directions is now bolstered by computerized navigoggles. These help him negotiate the tangled warren of overlapping alleys and thoroughfares of Olega City.

UL-413 SCAPER DROID

As Olega City lacks paved roads, it employs scaper droids to flatten and groom terrain to a state suitable for pedestrian and vehicular traffic. The civic scapers include models like this treaded UL-413, that employ traction fields to smooth and dry out dirt.

NOSLI'S LANDSPEEDER

Landspeeder traffic is rare in the oldest neighborhoods of Olega City, as the congested streets cannot easily accommodate vehicles. As a longtime resident, Nosli Tilbruk feels he can be an exception to this unwritten rule and drives his Mobquet C/L-22 close to the Jedi temple on errands.

Padded acceleration chair

Driver's side transparisteel windshield

Cooling intake grille module

Mobquet L-22AVA power core engine (under hood)

Integral radiant exhaust channel

Air cooling grille

FACT FILE

After Mae's escape, the Jedi lock down the city and place teams of Knights and local sentries at the city's entrances.

Olega City has a limited spaceport within its walls, so hired speeders provide transit to and from the outlying landing fields.

DATA FILE

MANUFACTURER Mobquet Swoops and Speeders

MODEL C/L-22 Karozzin

TYPE Landspeeder

DIMENSIONS Height: 1.4 m (4 ft 7 in); Length: 3.48 m (11 ft 5 in); Width: 1.6 m (5 ft 3 in)

SPEED 130 kph (80 mph)

WEAPONS None

AFFILIATION Independent

CHAPTER 3

THE THIRD TARGET

In the densely forested wilderness of Khofar can be heard the howls of a lone Wookiee. Master Kelnacca has transformed an outpost assignment into a time of exile and penance. A powerful Wookiee strong in the Force may be Mae Aniseya's most daunting challenge, especially since she must first survive the dangers of the untamed forest before coming within striking distance of her Jedi target.

KHOFAR

Low axial tilt, rich soil, and a slightly lower than standard gravity combine to give Khofar enormous forests. The planet is largely untouched by technology; it is protected by Republic regulations that keep business interests elsewhere. Visitors come to the planet eager to salvage the wreckage of failed charting expeditions. There is a small, underdeveloped tourism industry springing up to meet these needs, but for the most part Khofar remains unexploited.

DATA FILE

REGION Outer Rim

SECTOR Lahara

SYSTEM Khofar

DIAMETER 8,215 km (5,105 miles)

TERRAIN Dense forests, lowland steppes, mountains, and ravines

MOONS 1 (Khofeen)

POPULATION Less than 1 million

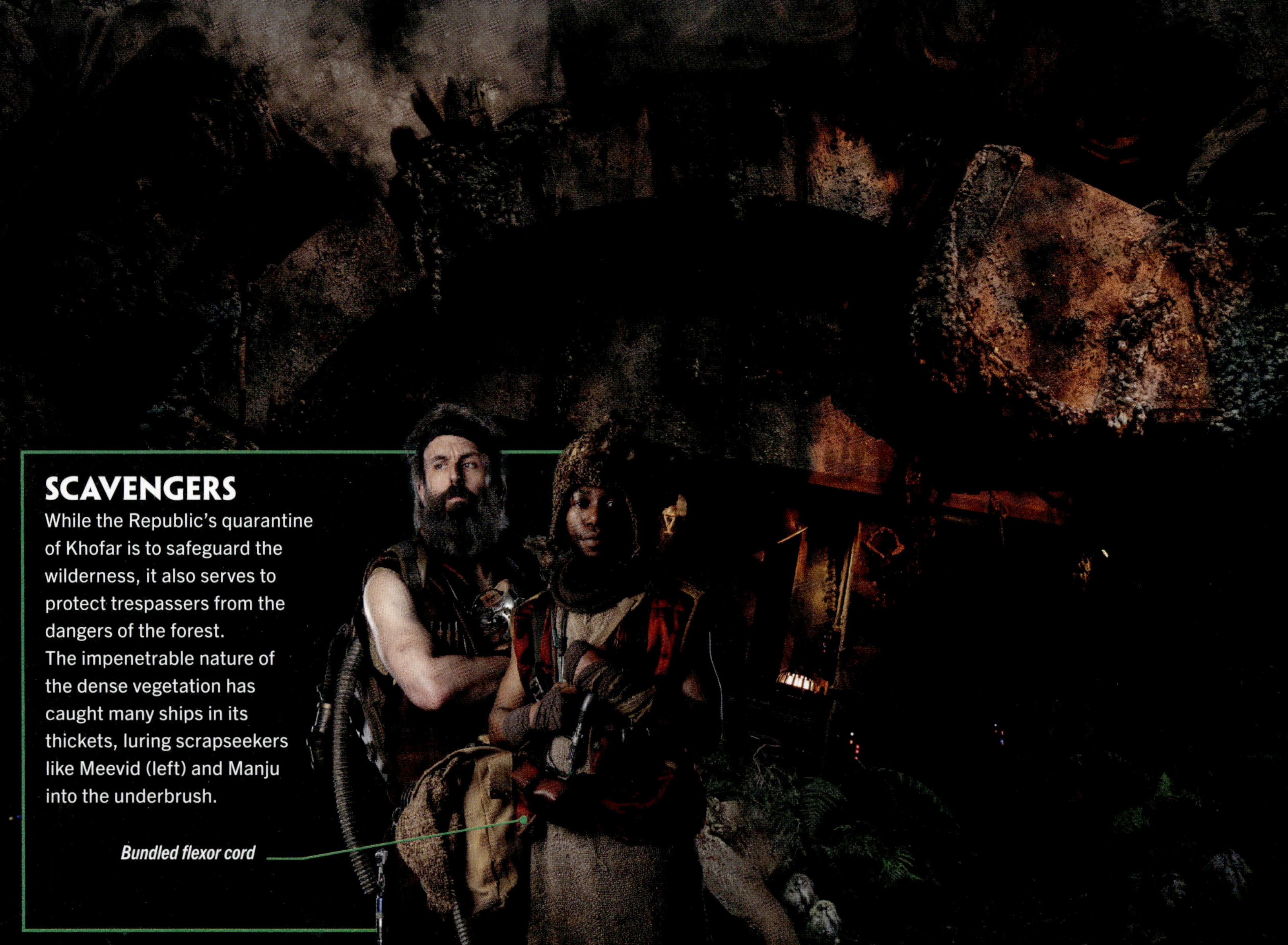

SCAVENGERS

While the Republic's quarantine of Khofar is to safeguard the wilderness, it also serves to protect trespassers from the dangers of the forest. The impenetrable nature of the dense vegetation has caught many ships in its thickets, luring scrapseekers like Meevid (left) and Manju into the underbrush.

Bundled flexor cord

EXPLODING SEED PODS

CLOUD DISPERSAL
The Khofar underbrush is dotted with a variety of colorful pods that explode when jostled, spreading their floating seeds into the winds.

GUMMY GREEN
The seeds of the virid trachiedo are coated in an adhesive, ensuring they stick to wildlife and are transported far afield before the gum dries out.

CHOKING HAZARD
The most dangerous of the pods are the orange crofax, whose wispy seeds can choke wildlife and then root within their carcasses.

YELLOW POPPER
The pods of the xan holicor are the loudest in the jungle, popping with a crack that can be heard for hundreds of meters.

UMBRAMOTHS

Among the most harmful predators in the forests are the umbramoths, nocturnal fliers that spend the day asleep, attached to trees and drawing in solar energy. They hunt at night, assisted by bioluminescence.

Chitinous thorax

Photosensitive compound eyes

Bioluminescent gut glows in territorial display

SPECKLED VERSIMILLIPEDE

Khofar is home to a particular variety of versimillipedes that exude a powerful poison through their spotted skin. Unwary travelers who are used to other, harmless varieties have died handling or eating them.

KELNACCA

A towering and noble presence exuding confidence and control, Kelnacca is a rare example of a Wookiee Jedi Master. His ancestry gives him a lifespan of centuries, which he has devoted to the study of the Force and his duties as a Jedi. Kelnacca knows the raw physical power at his command, and also the value of serenity. Wookiee reputations for short tempers are not without cause, but Kelnacca's mastery of his deepest instincts is expertly honed.

The vocal apparatus of Wookiees means Kelnacca cannot speak Basic, though he does understand it, and Shyriiwook is a difficult language for non-Wookiees to master. Regardless of this potential communication complication, the connection of the Force is there to draw Kelnacca and other Jedi closer together.

TIMELINE

Age 149	Assists in Starlight Beacon recovery mission.
Age 230	Witnesses the death of old age of his one-time Padawan Yarzion Vell; outliving companions is common for Wookiees.
Age 231	Completes the training of Padawan Ordea.
Age 231	Mission to Brendok with Master Indara.
Age 243	Assigned to Khofar by the Jedi Council.
Age 247	Ventures deeper into the forests of Khofar and loses contact with the Jedi.
Age 248	Killed by a mysterious attacker on Khofar.

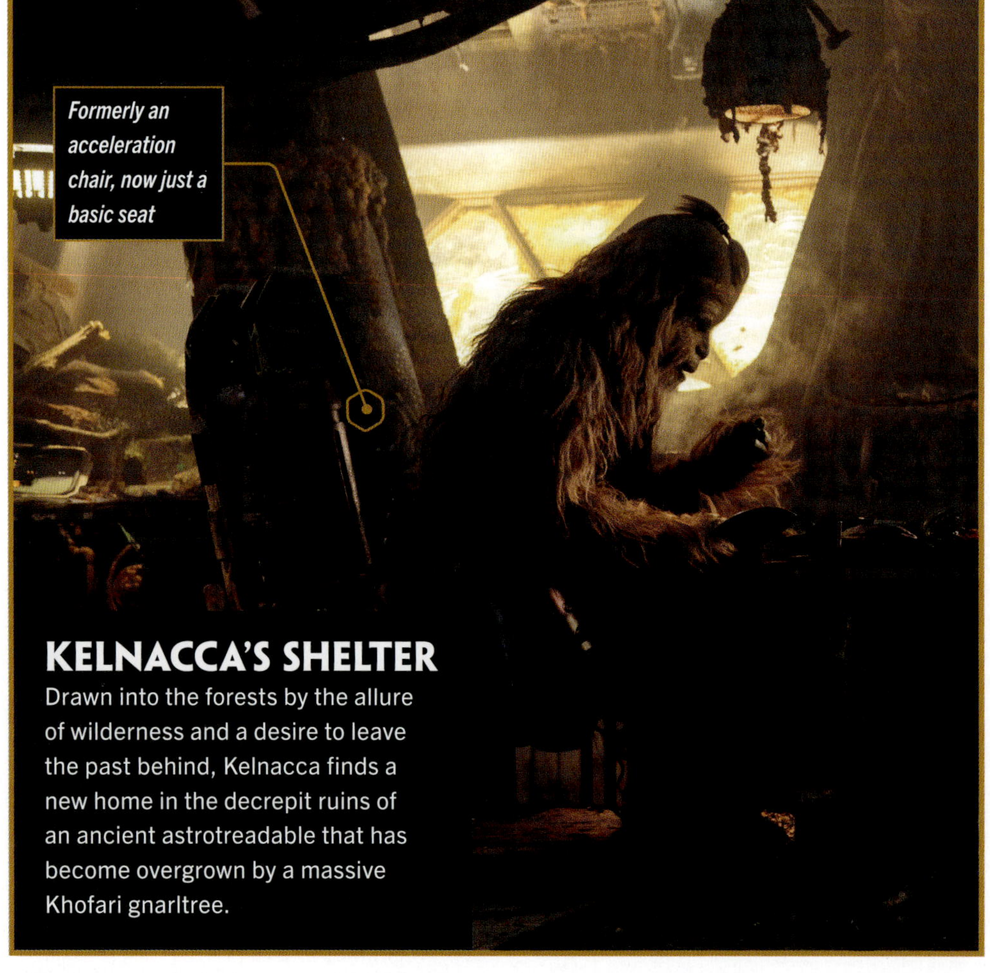

Formerly an acceleration chair, now just a basic seat

KELNACCA'S SHELTER

Drawn into the forests by the allure of wilderness and a desire to leave the past behind, Kelnacca finds a new home in the decrepit ruins of an ancient astrotreadable that has become overgrown by a massive Khofari gnarltree.

WOOKIEE JEDI

The physical prime of a Wookiee lasts centuries, and Kelnacca's well-honed physique pairs powerfully with Jedi disciplines. He has developed his leg strength to cover long distances and leap incredible spans as he traverses the wilderness-covered planet, Khofar.

Stance that can intimidate combatants into surrender

Muscled legs lend great power to Kelnacca's strikes and mobility

INTO THE WILDS

After finding Coruscant stifling, Kelnacca welcomed a posting on Khofar, a planet similar to his homeworld, Kashyyyk. The verdant surroundings opened his mind to the Force, and Kelnacca surprisingly abandoned his camp and instead decided to live as a recluse among some ancient wreckage. A sign scrawled in Shyriiwook warns trespassers to keep their distance, while Kelnacca lives off the land.

WOOKIEE SATCHEL
Kelnacca's traditional Wookiee satchel was a gift from a Kashyyyk elder. The bowcaster ammo loops can be used to store food supplies.

HORTICULTURAL SNIPPERS

KELNACCA'S LIGHTSABER

FACT FILE

An accomplished cook, Kelnacca can prepare meals fit for humans while on missions.

Kelnacca is obsessed with a swirling pattern that has clouded his mind for years since the mission to Brendok.

DATA FILE

SUBJECT Kelnacca

HOMEWORLD Kashyyyk

SPECIES Wookiee

AFFILIATION Jedi Order

HEIGHT 2.29 m (7 ft 6 in)

AGE 248 standard years

EXILE II

A slim craft with a silhouette that disappears at a distance, the *Exile II* is a covert vessel borrowed by Mae Aniseya in her system-hopping vendetta. The twin-pod tandem *Proa*-class ship is lightly armed and shielded, relying primarily on stealth for survival. A hyperspace docking ring stays in orbit during planetfall, its heavily encrypted navicomputer keeping its itinerary and port of origin secret. Mae typically operates the vessel alone.

DARK DESIGNS

A sleek Santhe Corporation design, the forked *Proa*-class was an exotic luxury craft produced over a century ago. The *Exile II* is battered and patched beyond easy recognition. The ship style has not been in service for decades, adding to its mystique and ability to defy identification. Qimir remains cagey as to its origins.

Outrigger boom holds long-range comms array

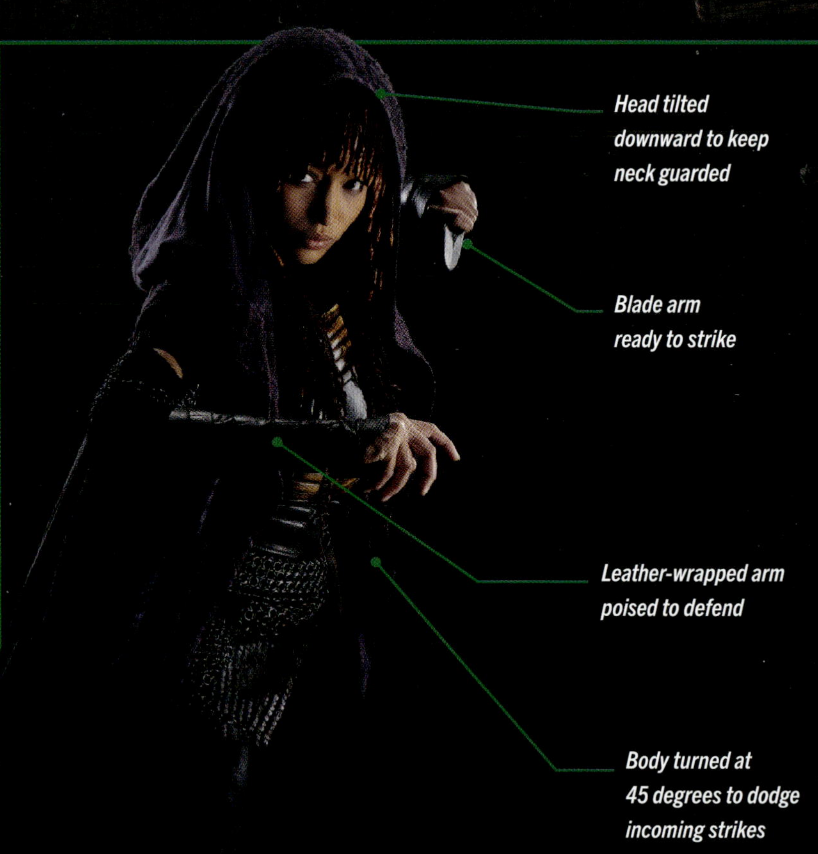

MAE ANISEYA

Having killed half of the targets on her vendetta list, Mae Aniseya has yet to satisfy the criteria set by her master: the unarmed murder of a Jedi. Qimir warns her not to stray from the master's command, but the discovery of Osha's survival is starting to sow doubts into Mae's obsession.

MAE'S CANTEEN

Mae takes care to conserve her energy after trekking through the Khofar forests, as her next battle is with a trained Wookiee Jedi Master.

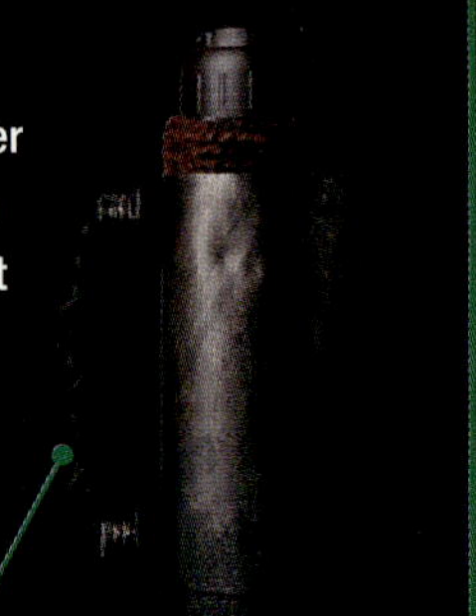

Improvised handle of cabling provides firm grip

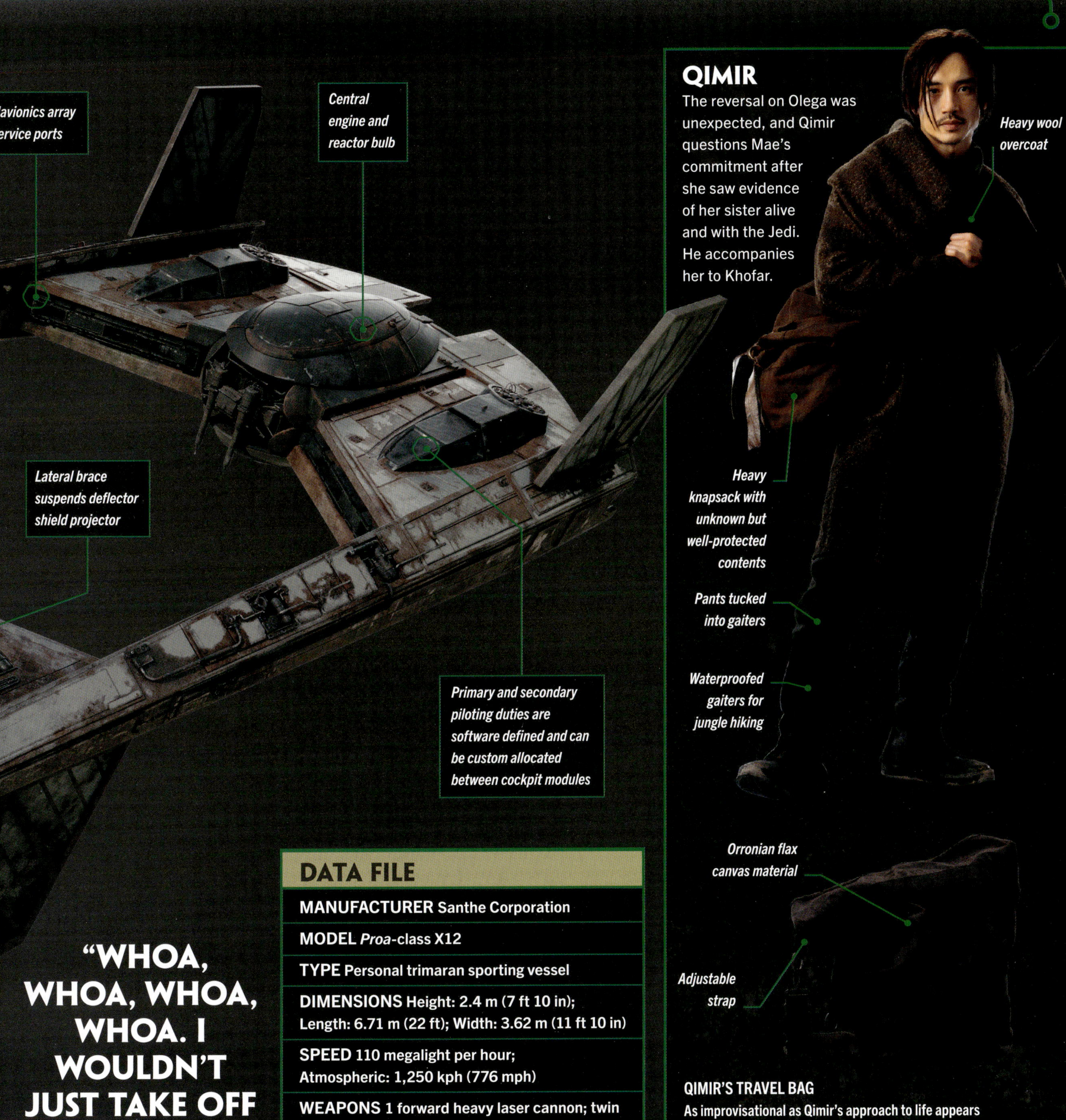

QIMIR

The reversal on Olega was unexpected, and Qimir questions Mae's commitment after she saw evidence of her sister alive and with the Jedi. He accompanies her to Khofar.

DATA FILE

MANUFACTURER	Santhe Corporation
MODEL	*Proa*-class X12
TYPE	Personal trimaran sporting vessel
DIMENSIONS	Height: 2.4 m (7 ft 10 in); Length: 6.71 m (22 ft); Width: 3.62 m (11 ft 10 in)
SPEED	110 megalight per hour; Atmospheric: 1,250 kph (776 mph)
WEAPONS	1 forward heavy laser cannon; twin downward medium laser cannons
AFFILIATION	Unknown

"WHOA, WHOA, WHOA, WHOA. I WOULDN'T JUST TAKE OFF IF I WERE YOU."
QIMIR TO MAE ANISEYA

QIMIR'S TRAVEL BAG
As improvisational as Qimir's approach to life appears to be, he does maintain a well-stocked go-bag ready for hasty escapes.

JEDI TACTICAL COUNCIL

As the criminal evidence—and Jedi murders—grow, Vernestra Rwoh convenes her own tactical council. The wary Jedi Master is concerned that vulnerabilities to the Order may be raised by unconfirmed leaks regarding the investigation. Vernestra compartmentalizes the information to reduce the chance that unscrupulous opportunists could use it against the Jedi. She keeps the High Council uninformed—at least, she reasons, until a clearer picture of the murky situation is revealed.

The Jedi Masters carefully examine the holographic recording that Yord Fandar captured on Olega, showcasing Mae's lethal fighting style that taps into awareness of the Force. That she is skilled is no question; just where she learned these skills is another matter.

"A SCANDAL LIKE THIS WOULD INSPIRE FEAR AND DISTRUST. WE SHOULD HANDLE THIS OURSELVES."

VERNESTRA RWOH

A COUNCIL CONVENED

The 10 masters Vernestra gathers are trusted advisors who she has worked with closely in her many decades as a Jedi. Sol is given a privileged position due to his direct experience with Mae, but authority rests with Veo Holden, who has the most seniority after Vernestra. Vernestra tasks Holden to organize a mission to Khofar in the hope of intercepting the killer.

Holden memorizes details rather than keeping an externalized record

Ki-Adi-Mundi's expertise has garnered the attention of the Jedi High Council

SECRET BRIEFING

The tactical council meets in a briefing room deep in the Temple, far from the more commonly traveled concourses.

KI-ADI-MUNDI

A newly elevated Jedi Master, Ki-Adi-Mundi is a Cerean with a binary brain contained in his elongated skull. Mundi is a contemplative master, though with a weakness for jumping to favored conclusions.

Lighter synth-leather belt
Ki-Adi-Mundi prefers the longer cut of temple tabards

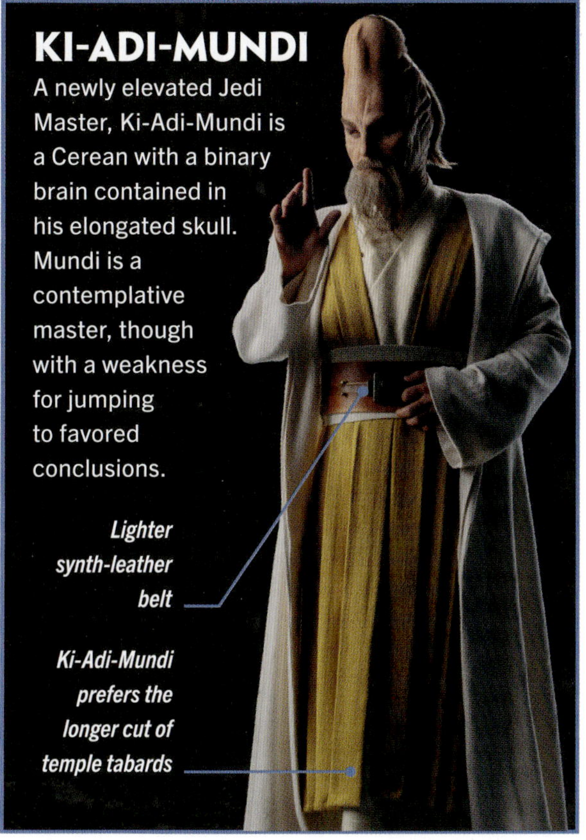

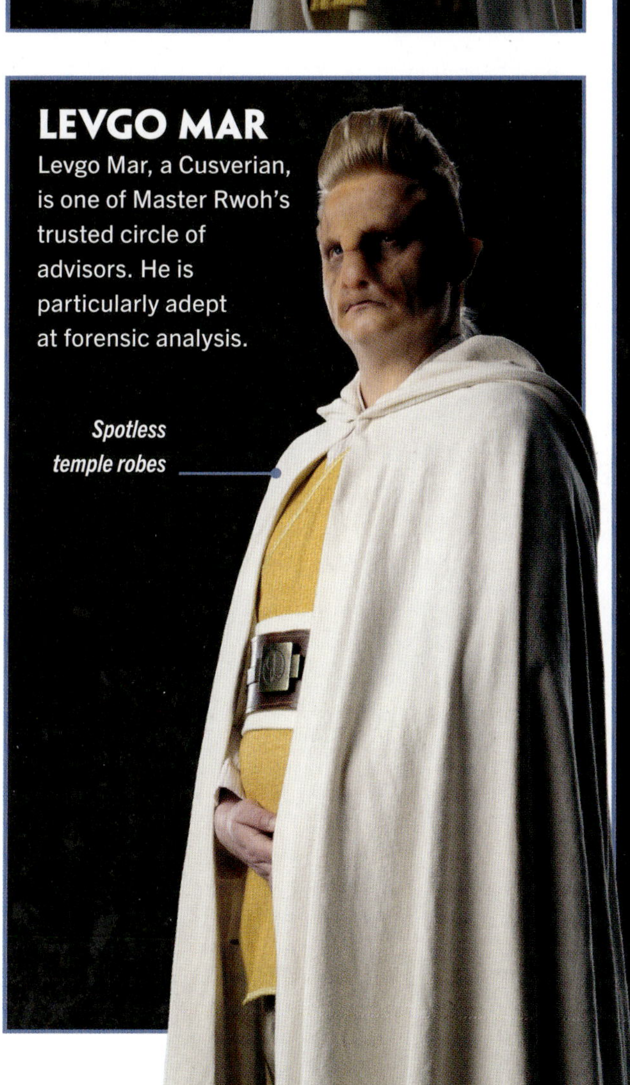

MASTER VEO HOLDEN

Examining the holographic recordings of Mae Aniseya, Veo Holden sees skill undercut by faltering emotional control. She has never seen anything quite like this and muses aloud that perhaps Mae is from some undocumented splinter order. Holden's next task is to assemble a team of Jedi Knights for the mission to Khofar.

FACT FILE

Though Holden has a stray thought that perhaps someone is attempting to emulate the long-dead Sith, she keeps the absurd idea to herself.

Holden worries that the mission may come to violence and so assembles a trusted team of skilled duelists to voyage to Khofar.

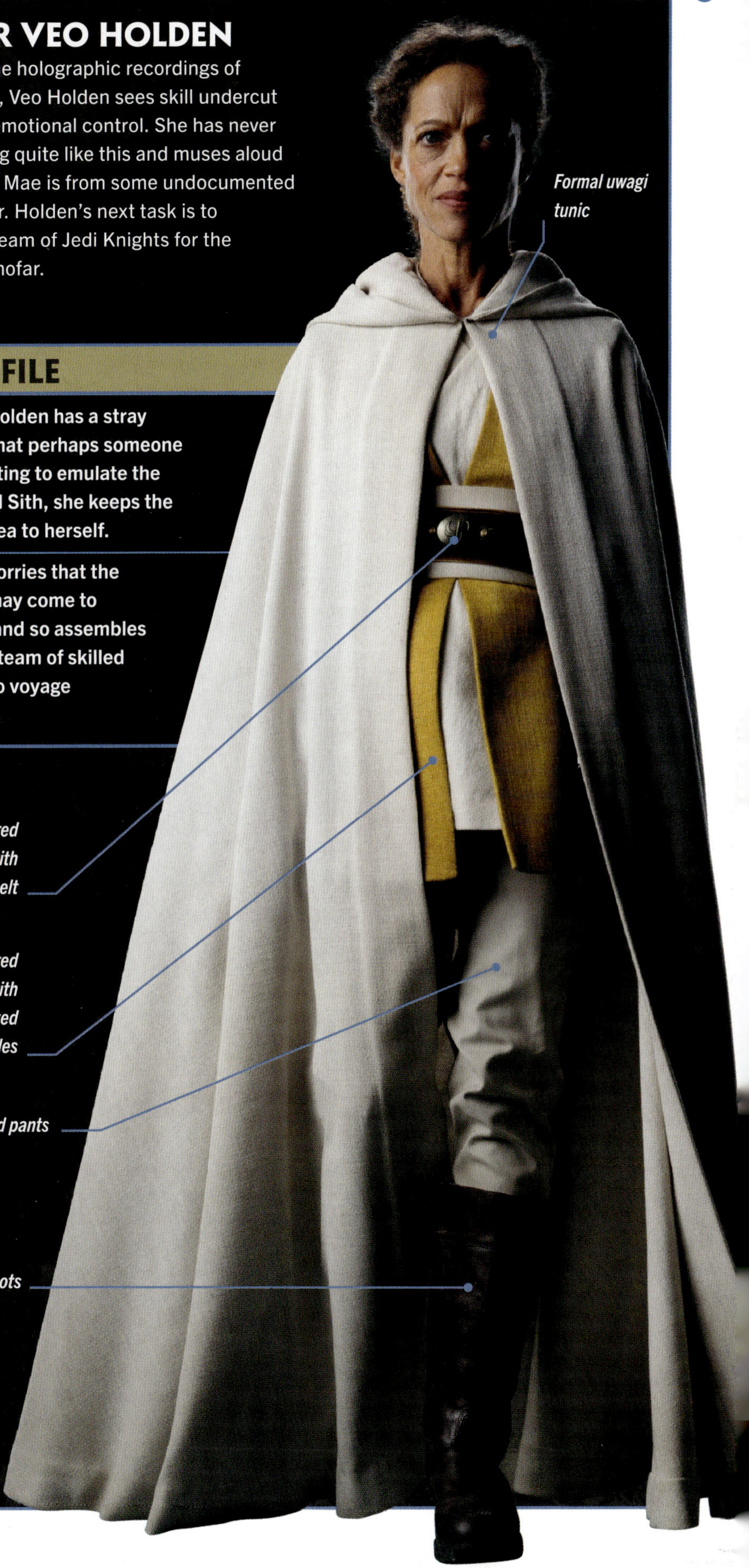
Formal uwagi tunic
Cream-colored sash topped with leather belt
Textured tabard with elasticized sides
Straight-legged pants
Calf-length boots

LEVGO MAR

Levgo Mar, a Cusverian, is one of Master Rwoh's trusted circle of advisors. He is particularly adept at forensic analysis.

Spotless temple robes

JEDI TEMPLE LANDING AREA

In this era of the High Republic, the Jedi Temple hums with activity, much of it originating from offworld. Spacers are commonly found in the Temple landing zones, either having traveled to petition the Order for assistance or having ferried a delegate from a distant world. The Jedi welcome the Temple being a crossroads of galactic citizens, since it keeps them connected to the Republic at large and not isolated deep in the Core Worlds.

"I NEED YOUR HELP. I NEED YOU TO COME WITH ME ON THIS MISSION."

MASTER SOL TO OSHA ANISEYA

DOCKMASTER DUTY

The Jedi Temple of the High Republic has enough non-Jedi traffic to require a staff of dockmasters managing through traffic, maintenance, and logistics. Mobile work stations let them situate to where demands are highest.

Tireless Selkath work ethic logs 18-hour daily shifts

SILVERTREADS

Commonly called "Silvertreads" by landing area staffers, the diminutive 2J-4DPR is a roving Lerrimore Automata astromech assigned to repair and assess ships visiting the Jedi Temple. Not only does it offer neighborly assistance to travelers, but it also surreptitiously scans for potential threats.

Upgradable ship systems knowledge cartridge

Standardized power cell

Portable dockmaster work station

Custodial droid keeps busy hallways gleaming

SPACEPORT TECH

PROTECTIVE CARRY CASE
This sealed duranium case with embedded diplomatic travel manifest-pad contains volatile coaxium vials in a shockproof repulsorlift suspension field.

Ancient "wind rose" symbol denotes pathfinding

TEMPLE DIRECTORY PAD
Simplified datapads are distributed to visitors to guide them around the Temple. The pads use holographic overlays for user-interface controls and information display.

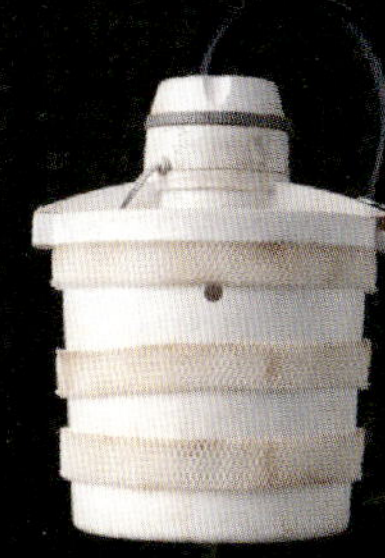

HORTICULTURAL CAMTONO
A protective travel container with a bio-key coded locking mechanism keeps rare plant samples safe for delivery to the Temple gardens.

COURIER HELMET
Space couriers push their navicomputers to the limit trying to coax even faster hyperspace transit out of established or newly blazed lanes.

LANDING ZONES

While the Temple spires house circular launch bays for compact Jedi Vectors and airspeeders, larger vessels lift off from public hangar facilities below the ziggurat overhang.

Overhang "hood" has pollutant-negating filters

The Polan departs on a Temple-specified skylane vector

HIRIM MITOKA
Messengers like Hirim Mitoka still find work with cultures and worlds with insecure transmission networks.

Regulation survival gear

PARABUR TULEG
Surface courier Parabur Tuleg makes runs across the city and into the lower levels.

Pressure-activated para-foil vest

PEEX CURANDO
Dockmaster and passenger service agent, Peex Curando fields questions about departure and arrival times and gates.

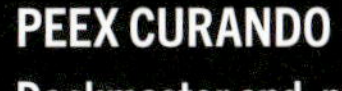

Atmospheric mister concealed under tunic

JEDI TASK FORCE

The murderous pattern becomes concerningly clear: Indara, Torbin, Sol, and Kelnacca. The targets of the elusive assassin share a common bond—a calamitous mission to Brendok 16 years earlier. Osha Aniseya has identified the killer as her twin sister, Mae. With Sol ensconced on Coruscant and Kelnacca living as a recluse on distant Khofar, all signs point to the Wookiee Jedi being the next target.

Veo Holden assembles a task force of capable Jedi Knights who will intercept and bring Mae to justice. There will be no record of this assignment, a peculiar move by Vernestra Rwoh, radiating more distrust than caution. Sol will lead the mission, with Jecki and Yord serving as lieutenants. Despite initial reservations, Osha joins the civilian contingent of the task force, offering her unique advantage of being the target's sibling.

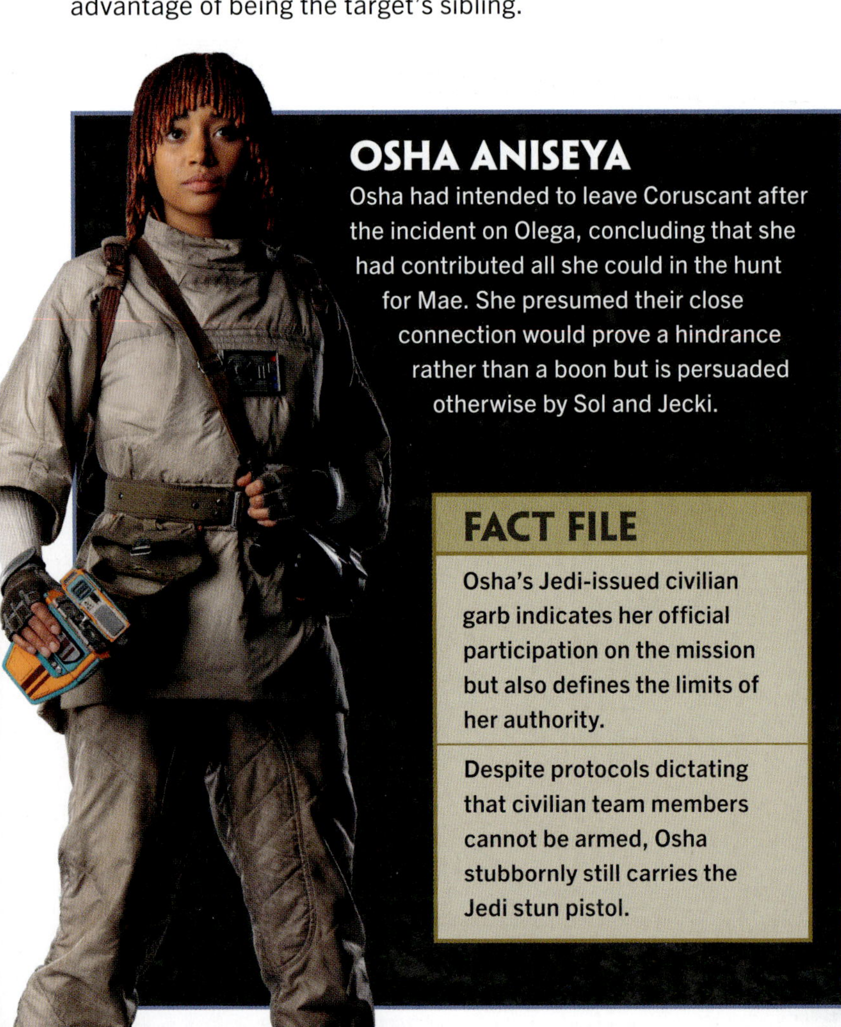

OSHA ANISEYA

Osha had intended to leave Coruscant after the incident on Olega, concluding that she had contributed all she could in the hunt for Mae. She presumed their close connection would prove a hindrance rather than a boon but is persuaded otherwise by Sol and Jecki.

FACT FILE

Osha's Jedi-issued civilian garb indicates her official participation on the mission but also defines the limits of her authority.

Despite protocols dictating that civilian team members cannot be armed, Osha stubbornly still carries the Jedi stun pistol.

WELLIG YUNS

Jedi Knight Wellig Yuns serves as a key member of the task force, observing judicial and Jedi protocol to ensure a valid arrest that won't be legally challenged. Though Mae has proven deadly, the Jedi seek to capture her alive for questioning.

Long-sleeved tunic

Dark shade of tabard for mission wear

Armored glove with durasteel plates

DATA FILE

SUBJECT	Wellig Yuns
HOMEWORLD	Moonus Mandel
SPECIES	Human
AFFILIATION	Jedi Order
HEIGHT	1.75 m (5 ft 9 in)
AGE	31 standard years

MISHA SHARUK

Jedi Knight Misha Sharuk has gained a reputation along the borders of Hutt Space for her tenacity and skill in tracking down law-benders in that raucous region of the galaxy. She is a skilled investigator.

FACT FILE

Bounty hunters have taken to avoiding quarries they hear Sharuk is interested in, as she invariably catches them first.

Sharuk has honed her specialist psychometric postcognition skills to examine evidence left at crime scenes.

SEN BENNEX

Jedi Knight Sen Bennex pores over criminal reports compiled from across the Republic, seeking out patterns and anticipating trouble spots before they grow unmanageable. He focuses on the pragmatic and preemptive application of Jedi authority to ensure peace and security.

FACT FILE

Bennex often works with Republic judicials in the field.

He is welcomed by many local authorities when he visits.

INRO JADREL

A combat instructor at the Jedi Temple, Inro Jadrel is a precise swordmaster who demonstrates impeccable control of the lightsaber blade, able to strike and disarm with nonlethal swipes of the otherwise deadly weapon.

FACT FILE

Jadrel regularly drills with combat droids set to maximum difficulty.

More than one Jedi trial has involved a Padawan having to disarm Jadrel with a training saber.

ITHIA PAAN

Ithia Paan serves as diplomatic liaison to the Baran Do sages, allies to the Jedi Order. The ancient sages are steeped in Kel Dor tradition and specialize in seeing the future. Oddly, they cannot get a clear vision of Paan's future, a fact that troubles the sage elders.

FACT FILE

Ithia Paan's own farseeing abilities are no more acute than most Jedi Knights of her training.

Paan's breather mask protects her from the caustic effects of oxygen on her Kel Dor lungs.

BAZIL

When it becomes evident that they may be dealing with a quarry who is gifted in the Force and deception, the Jedi opt to think outside the bounds of routine, requesting assistance from the local Tynnan embassy on Coruscant. A past associate of the Order joins the mission to Khofar. Bazil is a civilian ally who offers up his superlative olfactory tracking ability. The quirky tracker has super senses beyond even most Tynnans, allowing him to sniff out targets over dense and difficult terrain.

Both Jecki and Yord have seen Bazil in action before, either on field assignments or in visiting lectures at the Jedi Temple.

TYNNAN TRACKER

As an aquatic mammalian species, Tynnans are most at home in the frigid freshwater lakes and rivers of their well-maintained home planet. They are energetic beings with high metabolisms to keep themselves warm. Although Tynnans have been part of the Galactic Republic for many decades, Bazil himself is not well traveled and speaks only his native tongue.

Ever-fidgeting dexterous hands

Garb catches shedding fur in warm environments

Webbed toes aid in swimming

Armed with the scent from Osha's backpack, Bazil leads a Jedi team through the Brendok forests.

Though Tynnans themselves are a technologically advanced culture, Bazil is briefly confounded by a PIP droid.

Bazil's bulbous nose has more than 450 million scent receptors, and he has a remarkable sense memory when it comes to odors.

BAZIL

Bazil is eccentric for a Tynnan, a species generally regarded as gregarious and jovial. Bazil finds it hard to prioritize tasks and to focus on certain ones. Though his attention may be scattered, his results are reliable.

Dials for focusing goggles to compensate for poor eyesight

Jedi-issued civilian robe

ID module with Jedi authority codes

Utility belt with threaded satchels

Packed tracomp module

Synth-hide knee guards

Gaiters strapped over furred legs

"GREAT, HE'S VANISHED AGAIN. I SWEAR WE NEED A TRACKER JUST TO TRACK OUR TRACKER."
YORD FANDAR

FACT FILE

The comfortable, noncompetitive Tynnan society has state-offered necessities and amenities.

Tynnans are governed by lottery, with every citizen having a chance to serve in their legislature.

DATA FILE

SUBJECT Bazil

HOMEWORLD Tynna

SPECIES Tynnan

AFFILIATION Allied to the Jedi Order

HEIGHT 1.12 m (3 ft 8 in)

AGE 19 standard years

KHOFAR TRADERS

Visitors to Khofar are so rare that the planet maintains the most basic of amenities for travelers. The "spaceport," such as it is, consists merely of an automated relay signal leading to a cleared strip marked by dug-in lightposts. A battered generator tops off power cells while a dilapidated pump provides fuel of questionable purity.

Maintaining the ports are two Huwawan brothers who offer safety tips, map programs, and battered survival gear for credits or barter. In their younger days, the Kajok brothers worked as in-person guides leading tourists along the few trails that snake through the forests. Now aging—with creaking bones and sore backs as well as their fill of ill-fated thrill-seekers who wander off-trail—the brothers stay at their dockside tent and instead wish any new explorers the best of luck.

RUSTIC DEJARIK BOARD

Though the forests promise adventure and exploration, there isn't much to fill time with at the landing area, so the brothers play a low-tech, high-stakes version of dejarik.

TAIBIK KAJOK

The older of the two brothers, Taibik Kajok prides himself as having the sharpest business acumen. His face bears the scratch of a perturbed umbramoth from the last time he accompanied an expedition into the forests.

Self-launching emergency flare canister

Woven hat from raffu plant leaves

Rough fiber made from the stems of the Khofari iotii plant

DATA FILE
SUBJECT Taibik Kajok
HOMEWORLD Khofar
SPECIES Huwawan
AFFILIATION Unaffiliated
HEIGHT 1.78 m (5 ft 10 in)
AGE 52 standard years

WILTOO KAJOK

Younger and more ambitious than his brother, Wiltoo Kajok thinks their stretch of land on Khofar could be turned into something more than just a barren field. He envisions lodging, restaurants, and a proper port but has only dim awareness of property laws and what increased traffic would truly entail.

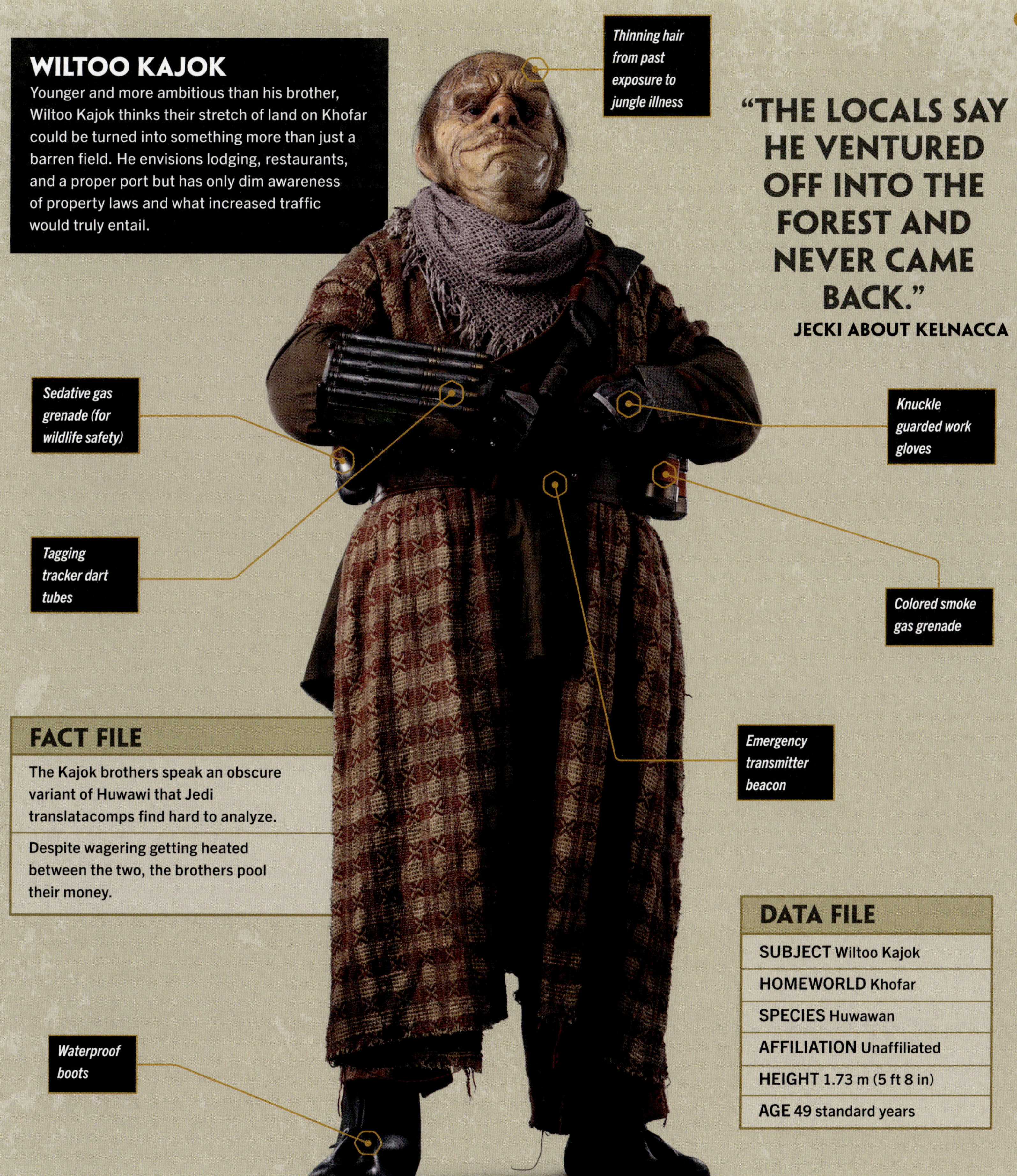

"THE LOCALS SAY HE VENTURED OFF INTO THE FOREST AND NEVER CAME BACK."

JECKI ABOUT KELNACCA

FACT FILE

The Kajok brothers speak an obscure variant of Huwawi that Jedi translatacomps find hard to analyze.

Despite wagering getting heated between the two, the brothers pool their money.

DATA FILE

SUBJECT Wiltoo Kajok

HOMEWORLD Khofar

SPECIES Huwawan

AFFILIATION Unaffiliated

HEIGHT 1.73 m (5 ft 8 in)

AGE 49 standard years

CHAPTER 4

THE DARKNESS

The Jedi task force surrounds Kelnacca's refuge in the forest, where Mae Aniseya has holed up. She makes a chilling discovery—her shadowy master is not only aware of her transgressions but has arrived to settle the matter. As night falls on Khofar, so too does a different, and far more deadly, type of darkness, wielding a red-bladed lightsaber...

THE STRANGER

Khofar's sun dips below the horizon, plunging the already shadowy forests into a deeper darkness. Master Sol's Jedi task force surrounds the entrance to Kelnacca's shelter, where Mae cowers next to the dead Wookiee's body. Her blood runs cold with the realization: her master is here and is aware of her failures and disloyalty, and everyone gathered at this standoff must fall to his blade.

Like a dark ghost, he drifts from the woods, tossing aside the Jedi with a blast from the Force that releases a cloud of spores from the undergrowth, obscuring his figure. The dust clears and his blade slices ribbons of red into the darkness, carving death into the Jedi Knights.

The evidence is unmistakable: the Sith live. But all witnesses to this revelation must die.

Weatherproof cape conceals physique

Integrated electronics disguise voice print

Muscular grip adds power to strikes

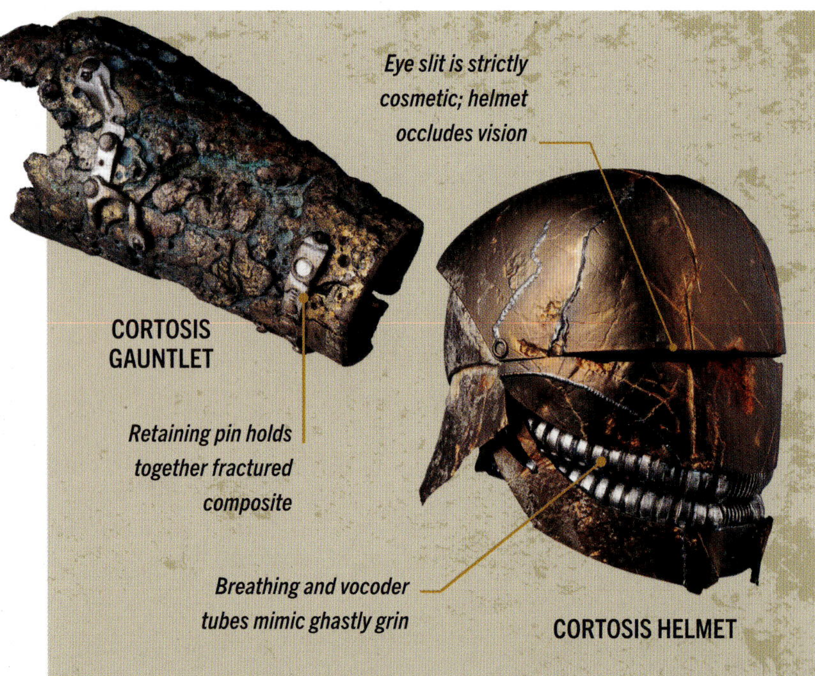

CORTOSIS ARMOR

The Stranger is clad in a battered helmet and gauntlet of cortosis, a rare metal with unique disruptive properties. The crystalline structure that grants it its effective conductive qualities also makes it brittle—the armor is prone to cracking upon impact. But its surprising ability to absorb and temporarily destabilize the kyber suspension fields of lightsaber blades makes all the difference in the Stranger's lethal attack.

SHADOWED LEGACY

The Stranger represents a disturbing throwback to a menace long believed extinct. He proclaims himself of the long-dead Sith legacy, popularly believed to have been conquered centuries earlier. His skills are indisputable, but whether he is the true heir to the Sith is a mystery no one will survive to solve, if he has any say in the matter. It is entirely possible he is a pretender to that lineage.

"I DON'T MAKE THE RULES. THE JEDI DO. AND THE JEDI SAY I CAN'T EXIST. THEY SEE MY FACE, THEY ALL DIE."

THE STRANGER

Vibrant red blade from corrupted kyber crystal

Firm control over fighting stance

Shoto blade in reverse grip

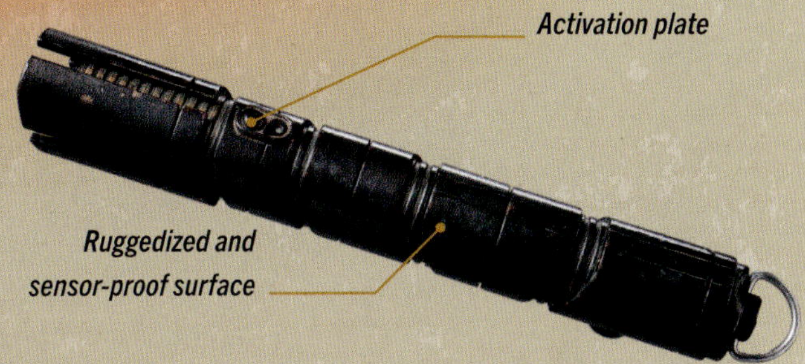

THE STRANGER'S LIGHTSABER

A SITH WEAPON

Mae's master carries a thick-handled lightsaber with a deceptive twist. The lower-section detaches to reveal a second, shoto-length blade. It's a secret the Stranger conceals until he can reveal it with deadly effectiveness.

SEPARATED LIGHTSABER

THE STRANGER UNMASKED

Jecki Lon lands repeated blows to the Stranger's helmet, cracking apart the cortosis shell to reveal a surprising face beneath. It is the man the Jedi and Mae have only known as Qimir—but that too is an alias. The Sith has no name, and the simple character of Qimir was an effective ruse that fooled even his closest apprentice.

DATA FILE
SUBJECT The Stranger
HOMEWORLD Unknown
SPECIES Human
AFFILIATION None
HEIGHT 1.82 m (6 ft)
AGE Unknown

SLAUGHTER ON KHOFAR

Although the Sith's lightsaber skills are underpinned by an unmistakable foundation of the Jedi arts, they are distorted by an unpredictable energy that unbalances the Knights. So focused is the Stranger's intense rage that it confounds their defenses. He lunges directly into enemy strikes to disrupt their lightsaber blades, and the Jedi are ill prepared to deflect such attacks. In short order, the Sith has killed all of the task force but Sol. Mae and Osha Aniseya also still stand to witness the carnage.

"YOU REALLY DIDN'T KNOW IT WAS ME, NOT EVEN DEEP DOWN?"
THE STRANGER TO MAE ANISEYA

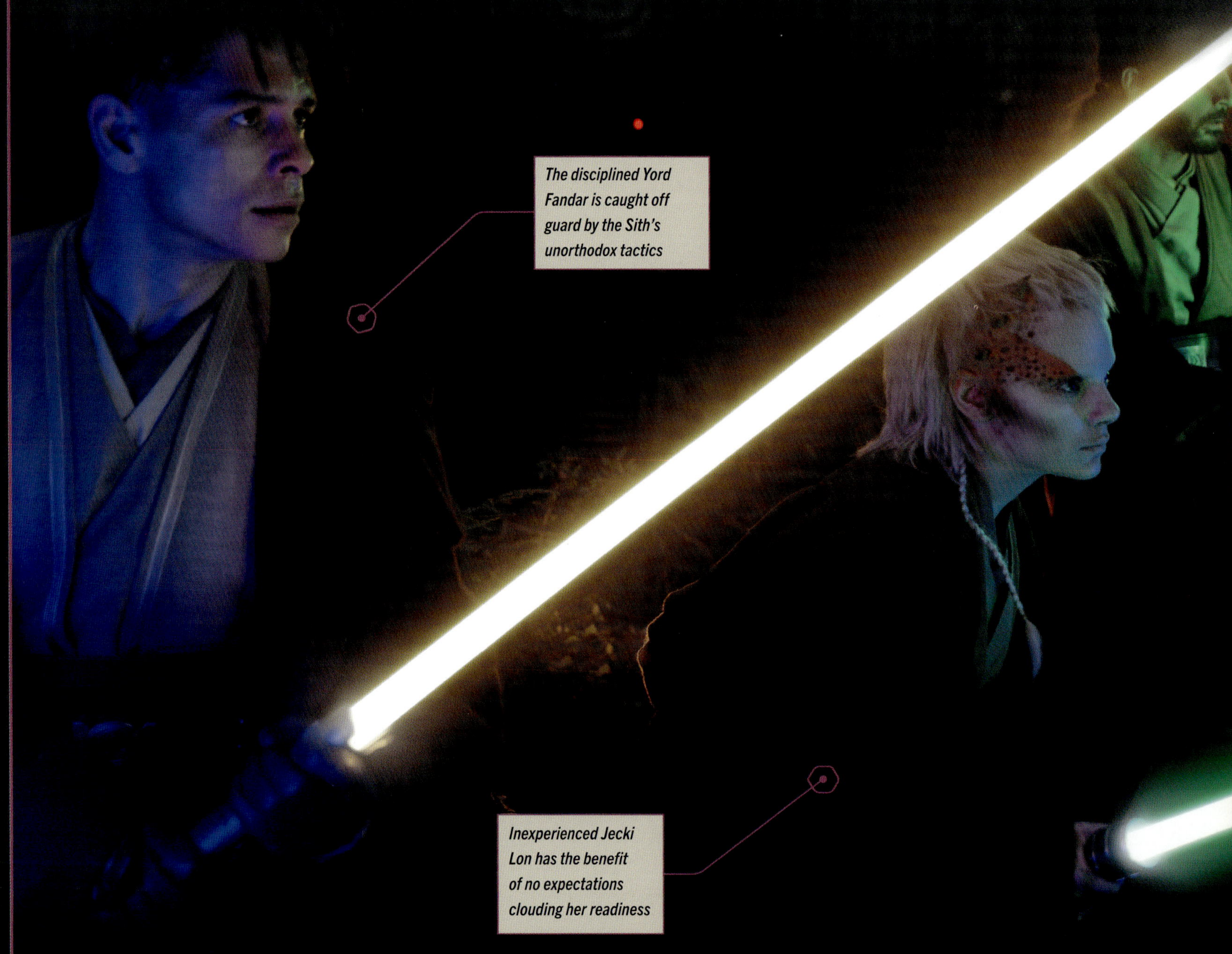

The disciplined Yord Fandar is caught off guard by the Sith's unorthodox tactics

Inexperienced Jecki Lon has the benefit of no expectations clouding her readiness

THE UMBRAMOTH SOLUTION

Recognizing the unbreakable tenacity of the Stranger, Osha attaches Pip's cognitive unit to the Stranger's back while in glow rod mode, drawing a swarm of deadly umbramoths onto the Sith.

THE SWITCH

Mae is marked for death for knowing the Stranger's face. She escapes Khofar by knocking her sister unconscious and adopting her identity. Mae shears her locs down to match Osha's hair length and departs with a stricken Sol. Though her pursuit of becoming a Sith acolyte has evaporated, she is still on a path to seek justice. Osha, meanwhile, is taken away by the Stranger.

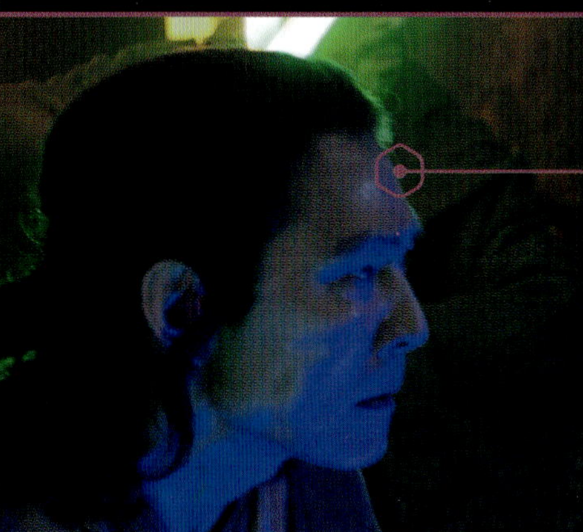

Seasoned Sol has never experienced anything like the onslaught to come

CASUALTIES OF KHOFAR

The details of the Khofar mission will be locked in the name of security, as well as deliberately misreported for other reasons.

What are chronicled are the known casualties:

- **WELLIG YUNS** Jedi Knight
- **MISHA SHARUK** Jedi Knight
- **INRO JADREL** Jedi Knight
- **SEN BENNEX** Jedi Knight
- **ITHIA PAAN** Jedi Knight
- **YORD FANDAR** Jedi Knight
- **JECKI LON** Jedi Padawan
- **KELNACCA** Jedi Master

Surviving the assault are:

- **SOL** Jedi Master
- **MAE ANISEYA** Wanted fugitive
- **OSHA ANISEYA** Civilian
- **BAZIL** Civilian tracker

DARK DESIGNS

His identity revealed, the Stranger proclaims his objectives. He wants to live free of Jedi persecution to wield his power as he sees fit. He wants a lineage that will survive him, by taking a dedicated acolyte who could continue his dark legacy. His justifications are well rehearsed, though rarely said.

THE UNKNOWN PLANET

After the carnage on Khofar, Osha awakens in the Stranger's lair, on a world missed by Republic star charts. It is a relatively young oceanic planet, dotted with island chains bubbled up from the depths by volcanic activity. An intelligent reptilian species lives far from the islands, but Osha sees no trace of them. The cave favored by the Stranger feels old yet functional, built around an exposed vein of cortosis ore. Osha sees evidence of Mae's presence—her daggers and clothes—and realizes that she is next in the Stranger's line of potential acolytes. Although she rejects everything he proposes, she cannot deny the conviction behind the words he speaks.

DATA FILE

REGION Outer Rim

SECTOR Auril

SYSTEM XA-1958JHR (Columi catalog system)

DIAMETER 11,570 km (7,189 miles)

TERRAIN Archipelago chains; vast oceans

MOONS 1

POPULATION Unknown; the world has a native population located far from the Stranger's island

Scrub foliage is common; larger trees are rare on these islands

Skura nesting ledges lead to deeper burrowing tunnels

Shingled surf zone leads to tide-covered tombolo

TIDAL LAIR

The cavern is separated from the landing plateau hosting the *Exile II* by a flooded plain, which effectively cuts off any plans Osha may have of an immediate escape. The Stranger recognizes that she is stranded with him and uses the time to talk and question her about her early Jedi training.

SKURA

Aside from birds and sea life, the island is dotted by nests of skura—tubby little vermingilua that feed off of stone fleas and formants in the seaside caves.

TERROR VISIONS

The Stranger's helmet is an exotic blend of cortosis alloys that not only offer electroplasmic protection against lightsaber blades but also serves to shut out the outside world like an isolation tank. With extreme focus, the Stranger can enter a meditative state while wearing the helmet, touching the Force. Osha dons the helmet and sees a terrifying vision of the future: Mae killing without a weapon.

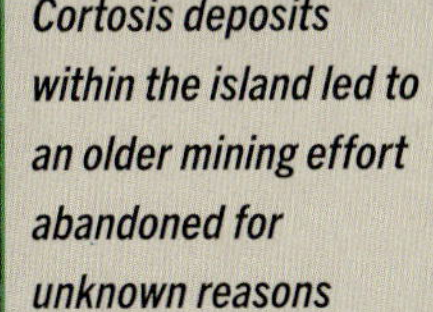

Cortosis deposits within the island led to an older mining effort abandoned for unknown reasons

DWELLER IN THE DARK

Aside from Osha and the Stranger, a third figure lurks in the shadows on the unknown world. The Sith Lord Darth Plagueis watches the others with great interest.

CHAPTER 5

HIDDEN HISTORY

The violence of the present is rooted in the tragedies of the past. Sixteen years ago, a Jedi mission to the mysterious world of Brendok made an unexpected discovery, unearthing a verdant planet that was home to a hidden coven of Force witches. But most intriguing were the only children found among those witches—a pair of remarkable twins with amazing potential.

BRENDOK

A verdant planet of forests and mountains, Brendok is a largely ignored world, the site of an old mining operation that was abandoned centuries earlier. Cataloged as uninhabitable, the planet became the covenstead, or sanctuary, for Force witches who had fled persecution. For years, they have lived in peace, moving into the old mine and transforming it into their witch fortress. Their scouts hunt in the fen beyond the mountains, and they stay ever vigilant to unwelcome visitors.

DATA FILE

REGION Outer Rim

SECTOR Wild Space (unincorporated)

SYSTEM Brendok

DIAMETER 15,321 km (9,520 miles)

TERRAIN Mountains and forests

MOONS 2 (Ashlasi; Bogaro)

POPULATION No official settlement

Mist common to morning and dusk, creates an ethereal feeling

Nutritive-rich moder humus layer of forest floor

THE HYPERSPACE DISASTER

Around a century earlier, a catastrophic hyperspace collision jeopardized worlds across the galaxy as lightspeed debris would emerge seemingly at random locations. According to Republic records, Brendok was one of the planets impacted, yet a routine inspection inexplicably shows the planet unharmed and vibrant.

BUNTA TREE

The name of the bunta tree is derived from the Huttese for "bountiful." It can be found on several worlds, but on Brendok the bunta tree flourishes like nowhere else. Its draping golden fronds give the tree a majestic appearance, incongruous with the toxic nature of the leaves.

BRENDOKI FLUTTERBY

The breed of flutterby found on Brendok is drawn to the nectar of the bunta tree and is able to metabolize its toxins. The soft-bodied creatures have membranous wings that flutter in a figure-eight pattern, letting them hover or glide along with the forest breeze.

Sturdy lunawood tree

WORLD OF SECRETS

As Brendok lies far outside the Republic borders, its history is undocumented beyond recordings from distant electrotelescopes. Its earlier settlers are unknown, and mossy ruins in the forests suggest there have been infrequent visitors across the centuries. The Force witches find the natural harmony of the world soothing, seeing it as an embodiment of natural polarities.

THE TWINS

The only children in the coven of witches hidden on Brendok are the remarkable twins, Osha and Mae Aniseya. Beloved by their parents, Mother Aniseya and Mother Koril, the siblings embody the future of the coven. A specific celestial alignment heralds the coming Ascension ceremony that will ready them for leadership, but not all is in harmony between the sisters.

As Osha grows and begins to define herself, she is more aware of the differences that separate her and Mae rather than the similarities that join them. Mae, by her nature, is more assertive while Osha is more introspective. Osha desires privacy, an idea strange to Mae, and while Osha's imagination spans outward, Mae's is firmly rooted on Brendok.

These disagreements come to a head as the Ascension ceremony approaches, coinciding with the arrival of Jedi explorers on Brendok. Osha knows little of the Jedi but is fascinated by them. Mae is wary of outsiders, a sentiment shared by the coven. To the girls, the Jedi are either an exciting portent of change or an ominous one of disaster. Tragically, they are both right.

WITCH HANDMAIDS

Handmaids Jala and Amsora ready the twins' gowns and hair for the Ascension ceremony. They tend to the twins together, as Osha and Mae do just about everything as a pair. Each handmaid has insight into each girl, with Jala watching Mae grow, and Amsora close to Osha.

MAE-HO ANISEYA

Mae-Ho Aniseya is the more aggressive twin, wanting to impose her will on her surroundings, whether it is as harmless as the path of flutterbies or as profound as the trajectory of her sister's life. Mae does not comprehend Osha's desire for independence, or the wonder she holds for the Jedi Order.

Hood can be pulled tight to protect against fierce winds

Leather double-strap belt with rounded brass buckles

Reflexes are primed to deploy a telekinetic block

Soft-soled boots give Mae a silent tread

DATA FILE

SUBJECT Mae-Ho Aniseya

HOMEWORLD Brendok

SPECIES Human

AFFILIATION Force witches (ascended)

HEIGHT 1.45 m (4 ft 9 in)

AGE 8 standard years (at the time of the Ascension ceremony)

VEROSHA ANISEYA

Verosha Aniseya is more prone to flights of imagination than Mae. Her notebook is filled with fanciful sketches, including those that incorporate symbols of the Jedi Order. Though Mother Aniseya is cautious to divulge information about the Jedi, every fragment stirs fantasies in Osha. She wants to express her ability in the Force outward, to the galaxy at large, and not just in the service of the coven.

Traditional ashoni locs

Straight-legged, dark blue pants

Tarandox wool shearling lined boots

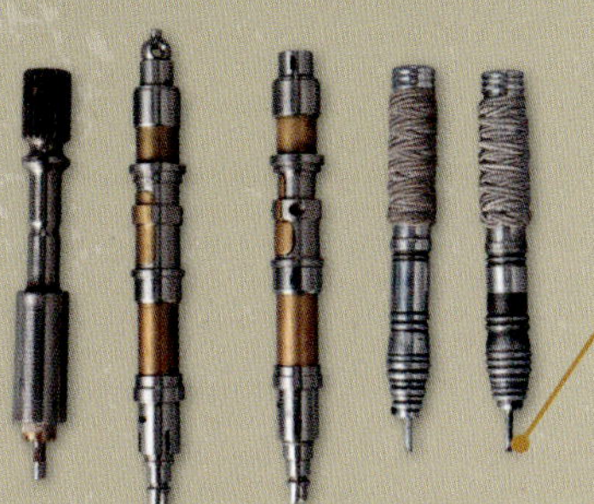

Carbon-tipped stylus

OSHA'S STYLUSES

In the vellum of her notebook, Osha etches fantastical illustrations, including aspirational images of the Jedi Order.

Coarse, tough, and absorptive fibers ideal for painting

ORBAK BRUSH

Osha uses this brush, made from the mane of an orbak, to participate in divination rituals by painting important runes on stones.

COMBS

Gifted to the twins from Ensign Rovi the ritualist, these sturdy combs are used by the handmaids to tend to the girls' tresses.

HAIR TIES

Osha handcrafts hair ties for herself and her sister using scrap notions from ornamentalist Ensign Eurus' haberdashery.

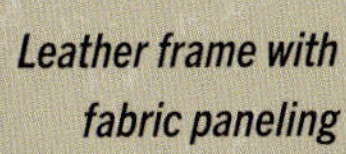

Leather frame with fabric paneling

Tumbler lock to keep bag sealed

SECRET SATCHEL

This handy satchel for Osha keeps her private items—like her journal—close to her and away from Mae.

Stuffed with willowbloom fluff

TOY TARANDOXES

Osha and Mae share this "family" of toy tarandoxes, based on a species found in the Brendok forests.

DATA FILE

SUBJECT Verosha Aniseya

HOMEWORLD Brendok

SPECIES Human

AFFILIATION Force witches (unascended)

HEIGHT 1.47 m (4 ft 10 in)

AGE 8 standard years (at the time of the Ascension ceremony)

THE MOTHERS

Leading the exiled Force witches is Mother Aniseya, with Mother Koril close by her side. Together they directly raise Osha and Mae, though the entire coven participates in the care and education of the twins. It was Aniseya who brought the coven to Brendok, finding sanctuary on the remote world. The witches harness and amplify the natural power of Brendok through their magicks.

Aniseya and Koril are wary of outsiders, given their persecution in the past. There are those who deem their abilities a threat—the Mothers include the Jedi in that group of potential enemies. When a Jedi expeditionary team approaches the mountain covenstead, at the very moment the celestial alignment of Brendok's moons ushers in the Ascension ceremony, Aniseya recognizes it as a major inflection point in the Thread of her life.

MASTER SCOUT
Koril's position of authority gives her command over the scouts of the coven.

ULTRASONIC WARSTAFF
Koril's antiquated warstaff uses ultrasonic generators to amplify the blade's cutting edge; its heft makes it an effective clubbing weapon.

MOTHER KORIL

As the more tempestuous of the handfasted couple, Mother Koril exhibits a more impulsive streak than her wife, Aniseya. She has cared deeply for the twins since the earliest days of carrying them in her womb. Koril sees herself in Mae's strong-willed nature and pushes Osha to be more like her sister.

Natural dermal striations enhanced and supplemented by ceremonial markings

Formal robes for Ascension ceremony

Dense velvoid pile fabric

Purple coloring attunes to intuitive magicks

DATA FILE
SUBJECT Koril
HOMEWORLD Brendok (adopted)
SPECIES Zabrak
AFFILIATION Force witches
HEIGHT 1.68 m (5 ft 6 in)
AGE Unknown

MOTHER ANISEYA

Using her wisdom and power, Mother Aniseya has guided the coven through hardship and tranquility, as she aspires for balance and harmony in her actions. She embodies patience, taking a long view in the preservation of her traditions.

Complex braids worn over shoulder like a scarf

Hands flexed for kinesic magick casting

THREADS OF DESTINY

Mother Aniseya describes the Thread of energy that outlines the shape of life and destiny to the twins. The quiver of this Thread shapes reality and can be manipulated and pulled along specific lines by a focused witch. It is a specific approach to the Force unique to this witch culture, standing apart from Jedi traditions.

Presentation platter with serving cloth

Striated blue skin indicates ripeness

KUIFO BLOOD FRUIT

A transplant to Brendok like the coven itself, kuifo blood fruit is often brought on long space journeys to keep the vitamin levels of the travelers at healthy levels.

Braids represent decades of growth and styling

Bustle skirt under robes

DATA FILE

SUBJECT Aniseya

HOMEWORLD Brendok (adopted)

SPECIES Human

AFFILIATION Force witches

HEIGHT 1.75 m (5 ft 9 in)

AGE Unknown

FACT FILE

Aniseya's jewelry is connected to ritualistic symbols and for enhancements of gestures.

Aniseya bears the mark of Ascension on her brow, having undergone the ceremony long ago when she was a little girl.

THE COVEN

Although the Jedi are the most prominent embodiment of those that can tap into and harness the power of the Force, they are by no means the only ones. In centuries past, Force exploration was represented by a rich range of philosophies, all united in discourse and debate in the Convocation of the Force. More recently, this coalition has waned while the Jedi continued their ascent in the Republic. Smaller disciplines still persist but are often branded as "cults."

Among those that continue to study and practice are a variety of self-described witches. Witchcraft has a long and strife-filled history in the galaxy and beyond. Though much remains obscured by the haze of time, there is documented research into the extragalactic Dathmirian descendants, the Nightsisters. This branch of spiritual evolution generated a wide variety of offshoot disciplines, including the coven of Force witches that would settle upon Brendok. These witches are not Nightsisters; they are their own school of thought and study. But they wield power enough to draw the Jedi's scrutiny.

ENSIGN SHIMA

Ensign Shima is the symbologist of the coven, keeping alive knowledge of how to etch and paint a wide range of potent symbols in places of power in and around the fortress. She carefully eyes the symbols of the visiting Jedi, examining the sweep and point of the Jedi crest.

ENSIGN EURUS

To assist in the gestural channeling of the Thread, Ensign Eurus is the coven's ornamentalist, creating fobs, jewelry, and other small talismans. A trusted advisor to Aniseya, she respects her leader's wisdom, although disagrees with allowing the Jedi's scrutiny.

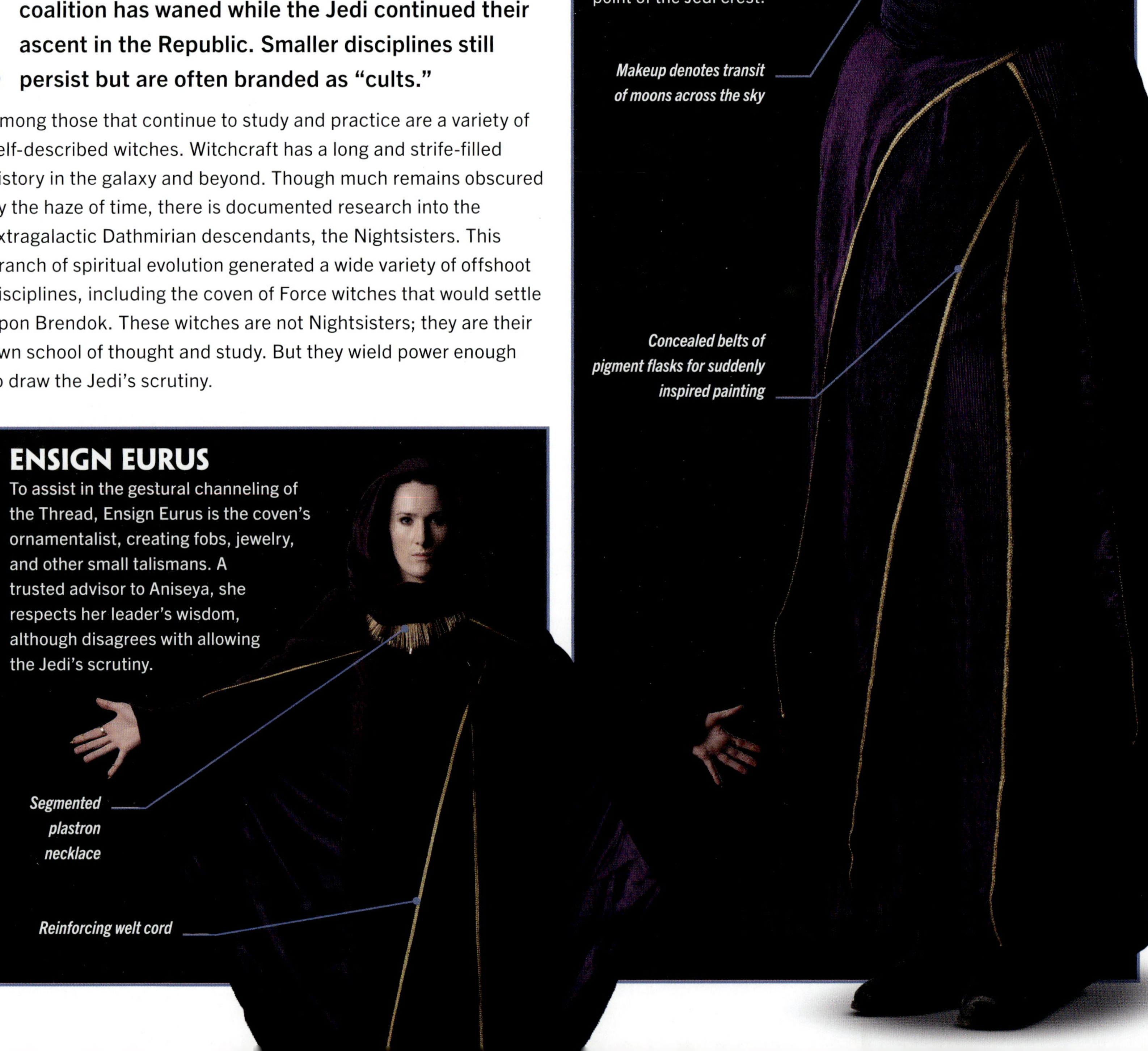

ENSIGN THERA

The coven has drawn adherents from several cultures during its travels, including the Twi'lek Thera. She specializes in healing and herbalism, tending to the sick and wounded.

Head-tails decorated with concentric orbit patterned "leklets"
Leggings conceal dagger

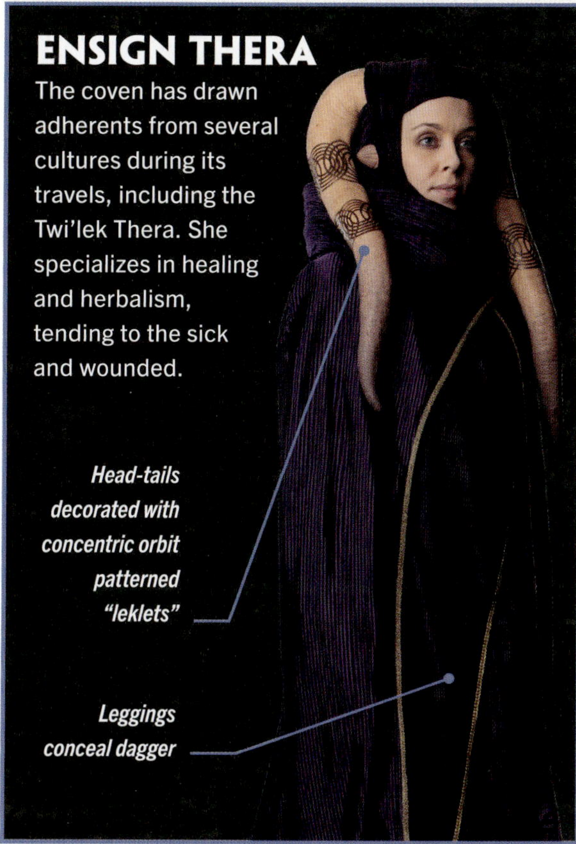

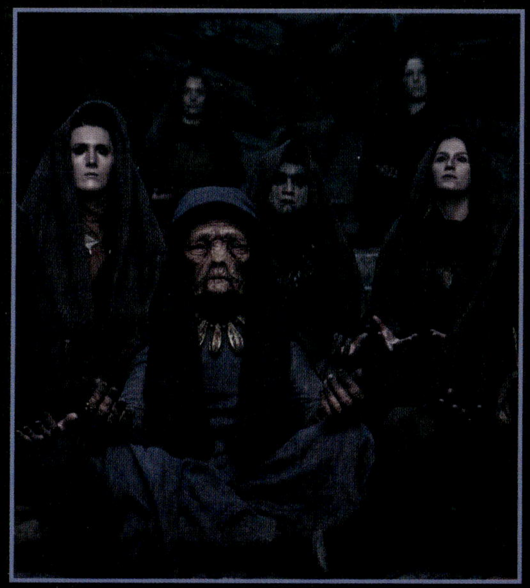

THE COVEN ENSIGNS
An estimated 54 witches live in the covenstead. The ensigns are named for being the bearers of ancient standards in specialized areas of the craft, such as astrologer, tapissier, numerologist, chorister, scrivener, and alchemist. The term "sister" is the most common informal title used among the witches when ceremony does not dictate proper ranks.

ELDER NAASA

Believed to be the oldest of the witches, Elder Naasa is the coven's augur. She is able to divine visions of the future by examining and extrapolating vibrations along the Thread. Her deep knowledge and experience give her insight to put these visions into context. Her divination skills are cherished by Mother Aniseya, but Naasa respectfully provides options and insights, not directives.

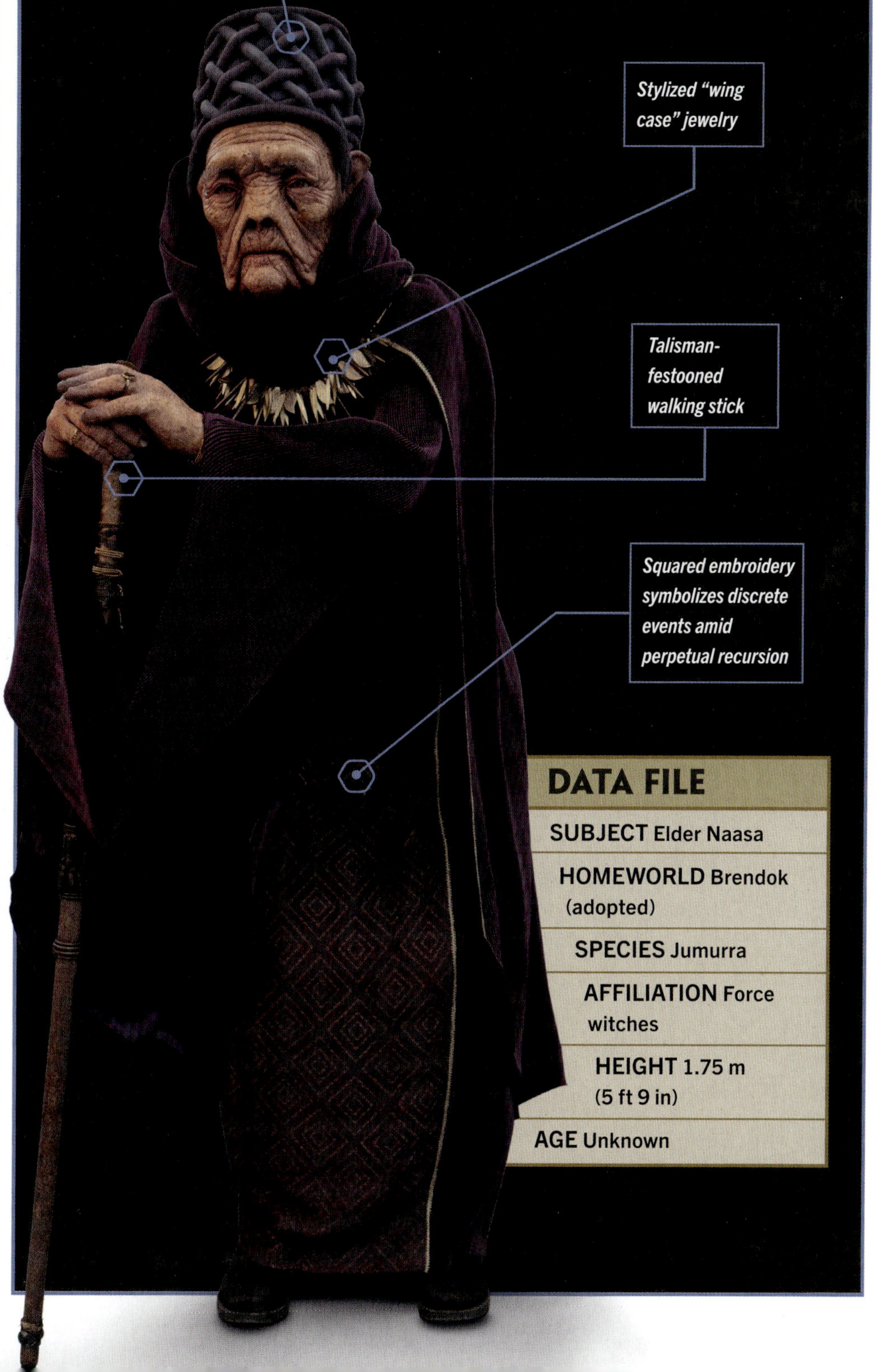

Densely corded turban symbolizes intricacy of thought
Stylized "wing case" jewelry
Talisman-festooned walking stick
Squared embroidery symbolizes discrete events amid perpetual recursion

DATA FILE
SUBJECT Elder Naasa
HOMEWORLD Brendok (adopted)
SPECIES Jumurra
AFFILIATION Force witches
HEIGHT 1.75 m (5 ft 9 in)
AGE Unknown

THE SCOUTS

The witch scouts are tasked with the protection of the mountain fortress and the exploration of its surrounding territory for potential threats. They also hunt and forage beyond the fortress walls, bringing back foodstuffs and other essentials. The scouts have the ability to tap into the power of the Thread, but their focus tends to emphasize an awareness of surroundings—they are the most vigilant of the witches.

Only the scouts are allowed to range freely outside the fortress. Any other witches wishing to explore must have the scouts' permission, and are often escorted. It is impossible for a scout to become lost in the wilderness as they track the lands with an innate sense of navigation, attuned to the orbital positions of Brendok's moons. In the summer, they actively hunt tarandoxes and other animals for meat, bone, sinews, and hides. In the winter, they use the poison of the bunta tree in traps.

SCOUT UMUR

Feeling most at home within the mountains, Scout Umur can free-climb some of the sheerest cliffs to ascend to the highest vantage point. She was the first to spot the arriving Jedi ship and reported it to Mother Aniseya.

Corded braid grown for nine winters

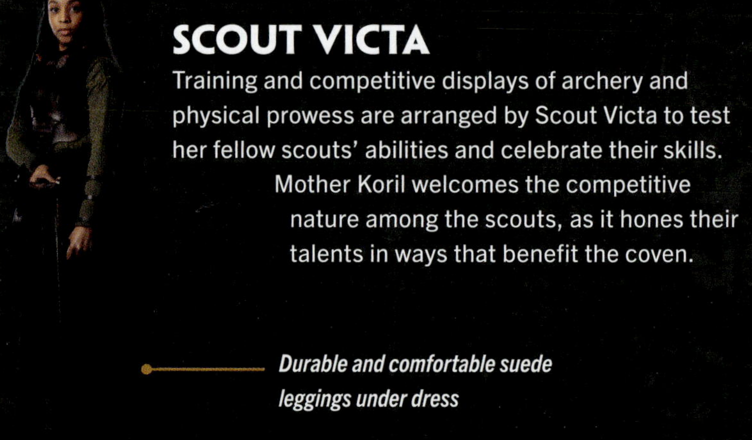

SCOUT VICTA

Training and competitive displays of archery and physical prowess are arranged by Scout Victa to test her fellow scouts' abilities and celebrate their skills. Mother Koril welcomes the competitive nature among the scouts, as it hones their talents in ways that benefit the coven.

Durable and comfortable suede leggings under dress

SCOUT ZAPALA

Zapala patrols the wetlands south of the fortress, in the marshes that provide drinking holes for a wide variety of wildlife. She is a skilled angler and often returns with fish for the cooks to prepare.

Functional necklace with braided lodestones

Fletching colors include wine red, mid brown, and green

Leather quiver holds five arrows

SCOUT KRUNA

Her synchronicity with the Thread gives Scout Kruna unparalleled visualization skills. Kruna is the scouts' mapmaker, with the ability to translate her travels into faultless illustrations that she shares with the coven's artisans to become the foundations of sprawling tapestries and electronic maps.

Optic pulse rangefinder mounted on riser

SCOUT SARRIA

The highest-ranking scout who reports to Koril, Sarria is a trusted guardian. Her affinity for nature aligns her to such a degree that she says she converses with the forests and can see through the eyes—and in some cases, direct the paths—of animals. Sarria interrupts the Ascension ceremony to bring word of the brazen Jedi trespass. With Koril's permission, Sarria and her scouts draw arms when the encounter grows hostile.

Tattooed Tosarvi lekku

Mounted ballistic weather reader

Lunawood riser

SCOUT'S MOON BOW

The arrows are tipped with crystalline moonstone fragments that the scouts can track by the power of the Thread.

Leather cuirass

Synthetic bowstring with 45 kg (99 lb) tensile strength per strand

"WITCHES! ARM YOURSELVES!"

MOTHER KORIL TO THE SCOUTS

Quiver worn at the waist or over the shoulder

Flame-tempered lunawood arrow shaft

FACT FILE

When the tense dispute with the visiting Jedi becomes unsolvable, Sarria and her best scouts unleash a volley of arrows against the intruders.

In combat, the scouts often conceal their faces behind a mask—a tradition Mae later emulates during her vendetta.

DATA FILE

SUBJECT Sarria

HOMEWORLD Brendok (adopted)

SPECIES Tosarvi

AFFILIATION Force witches

HEIGHT 1.7 m (5 ft 7 in)

AGE Unknown

WITCH FORTRESS

Long ago, an offworld mining concern came to harvest metals from Brendok, far from the prying eyes of the Republic. This rapacious entity dug deep into the planet's crust, seeking ores permeated with crystalline meteorite deposits that had fallen from Brendok's unusual moons. Something in the depths caused the miners to abandon the world altogether, and they vanished, leaving their technology behind. Their mountain mining installation was left untouched, ready for the witches to settle there and transform it into their fortress.

FACT FILE

Decrepit signage reads "Mount Mopu." This may be the mountain's original name, or it may derive from "mining operation processing unit."

Although the generator complex could theoretically function for centuries, neglect has made it dangerously unstable.

THE WELL OF DESCENSION

Balance requires the ritual of Ascension to be countered by a corresponding descent. This need is met by the deep borehole drilled into the planet. Master Sol reasons that the Force vergence on Brendok may be within the pit, its opposite pole defined by the converged moons. The ritual serves as a fulcrum between them.

GENERATOR ANNEX

The fortress' cyclic cryo-fusion generator is suspended above a temperature-controlling air shaft within the mountain. The outbreak of an uncontrolled fire throws off the cooling systems within the reactor, tipping off a cascade of explosions and critical malfunctions. After centuries of operation, the reactor explodes.

COMMON ROOM

Deep in the mountain adjacent to the reactor control systems is a spacious common room used by the witches for gathering, ritual, and training. Mother Aniseya prefers to lead at eye level, among scouts and ensigns rather than from an elevated command position or lofty throne.

Suspended mine control center, ignored by the witches

Retaining wall hewed from the mountain rock

Fatalwa crest

WITCH MOUNTAIN

Brendok planetary records are sparse, but a few proper names have survived. While mountain ranges are labeled—the range containing the covenstead is cataloged as the Fatalwa Mountains—individual summits remain unnamed. The highest peak once held a large deposit of lunar crystalline compress, an orogen thrust from the deeper crust.

THE ASCENSION CEREMONY

The Thread that permeates Brendok describes a perfect geometry of power, a triangulation of energies that meet the occult needs of the Force witches. The twin moons form a heavenly dyad that, when in conjunction with the exposed heart of Brendok, vibrates with an intensity that a skilled witch can harness. As the lunar eclipse reaches totality, Mother Aniseya harmonizes with the coven to channel this energy into her awaiting children.

"ASCENSION IS ABOUT WALKING THROUGH FEAR. IT IS ABOUT SACRIFICING A PART OF YOURSELF. THE POWER OF MANY INSTEAD OF THE POWER OF ONE."

MOTHER ANISEYA

Harmonizing coven enhances the Mother's channeling

Hooded guides mark the boundaries of the ceremony

CEREMONIAL STAFF

The Ascension ceremony has not been performed since the exile of the witches to Brendok. The Ensigns bring a variety of traditional trappings to maximize the impact of the event. Witch artifacts are marked with symbols of duality—twinned spheres in close orbit, as well as conductive planes that direct magickal energies.

Purple fabric dates back to before Brendok exile

Repurposed starship sensor probe as staff base

MAE'S ASCENSION

Mae is drawn to the promise of power inherent in the Ascension. At only eight years old, many of the symbolic nuances are lost on her. Mae's inability to accurately describe the ritual in detail leads the Jedi to presume the worst.

Velvet gown in ceremonial purple hue

Rare auroweave pleat forms ceremonial gorget

OSHA'S REJECTION

Osha's Ascension is interrupted by the arrival of the Jedi, a disruption she secretly welcomes. Osha wishes to have her own life separate from Mae and the coven, and the Jedi represent a truly viable alternative path for her destiny.

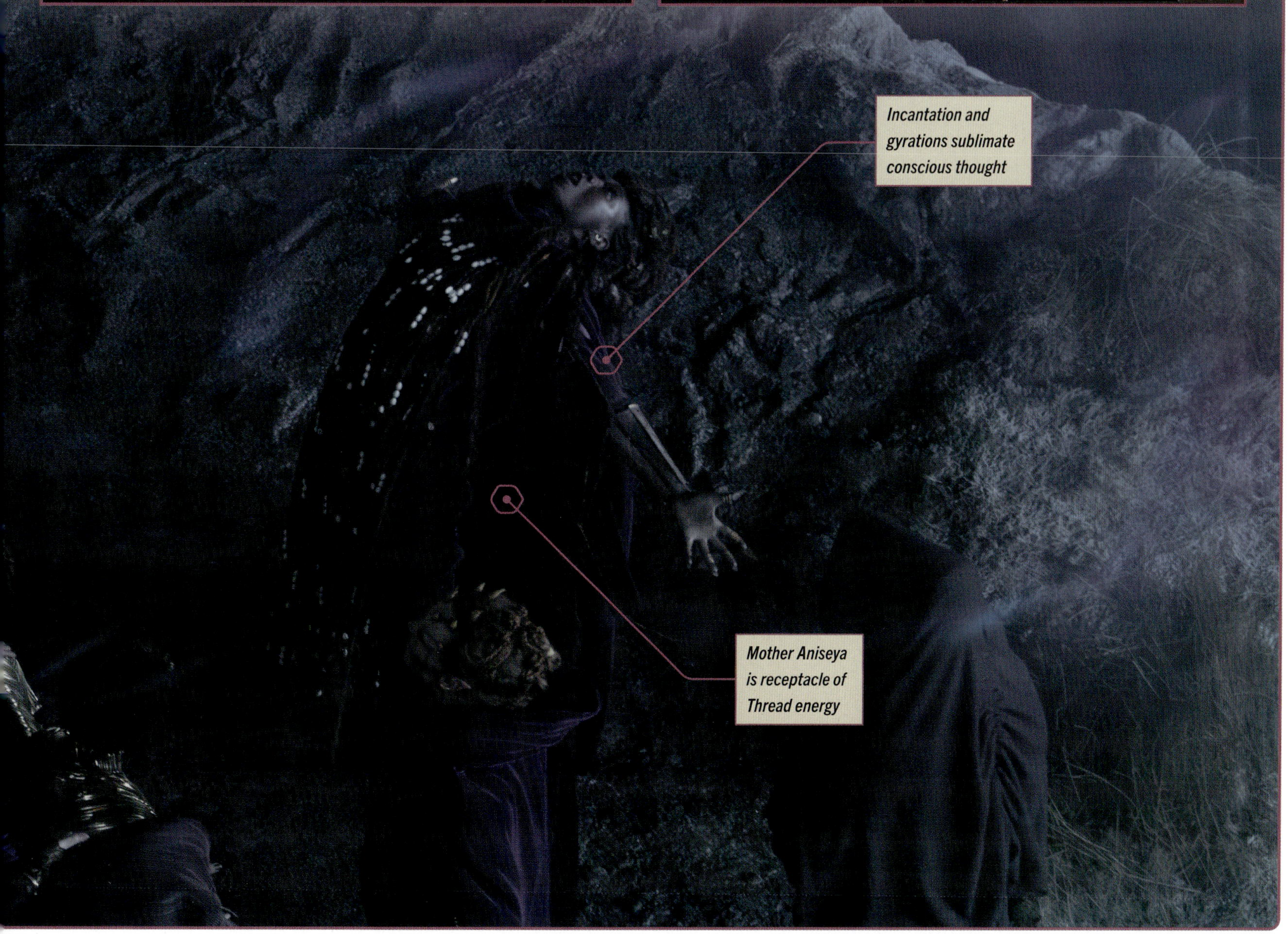

Incantation and gyrations sublimate conscious thought

Mother Aniseya is receptacle of Thread energy

JEDI MISSION TO BRENDOK

Over a century ago, notorious marauders known as the Nihil engineered a hyperspace disaster that detonated a ship as it traveled at superluminal velocities, scattering fragments of debris far and wide across the galaxy. Most pieces decelerated harmlessly into empty space, but enough wreckage kept tumbling through the curvature of hyperspace to pose an impact threat to inhabited worlds.

The Republic and Jedi Order worked diligently to plot the paths of any wayward fragments and anticipate Emergences—exit points of high velocity debris—so they could either intercept them or evacuate anyone in danger. Brendok was, at least according to records, sundered by an impact, but the Jedi Archives hold no firsthand accounts of the incident. It was an uninhabited planet far beyond Republic borders and was deprioritized. A century later, a wayward probe scan indicated the planet was inexplicably thriving with life. The Jedi Council dispatched a team to confirm these readings and gather any samples of living material that could explain this contradiction.

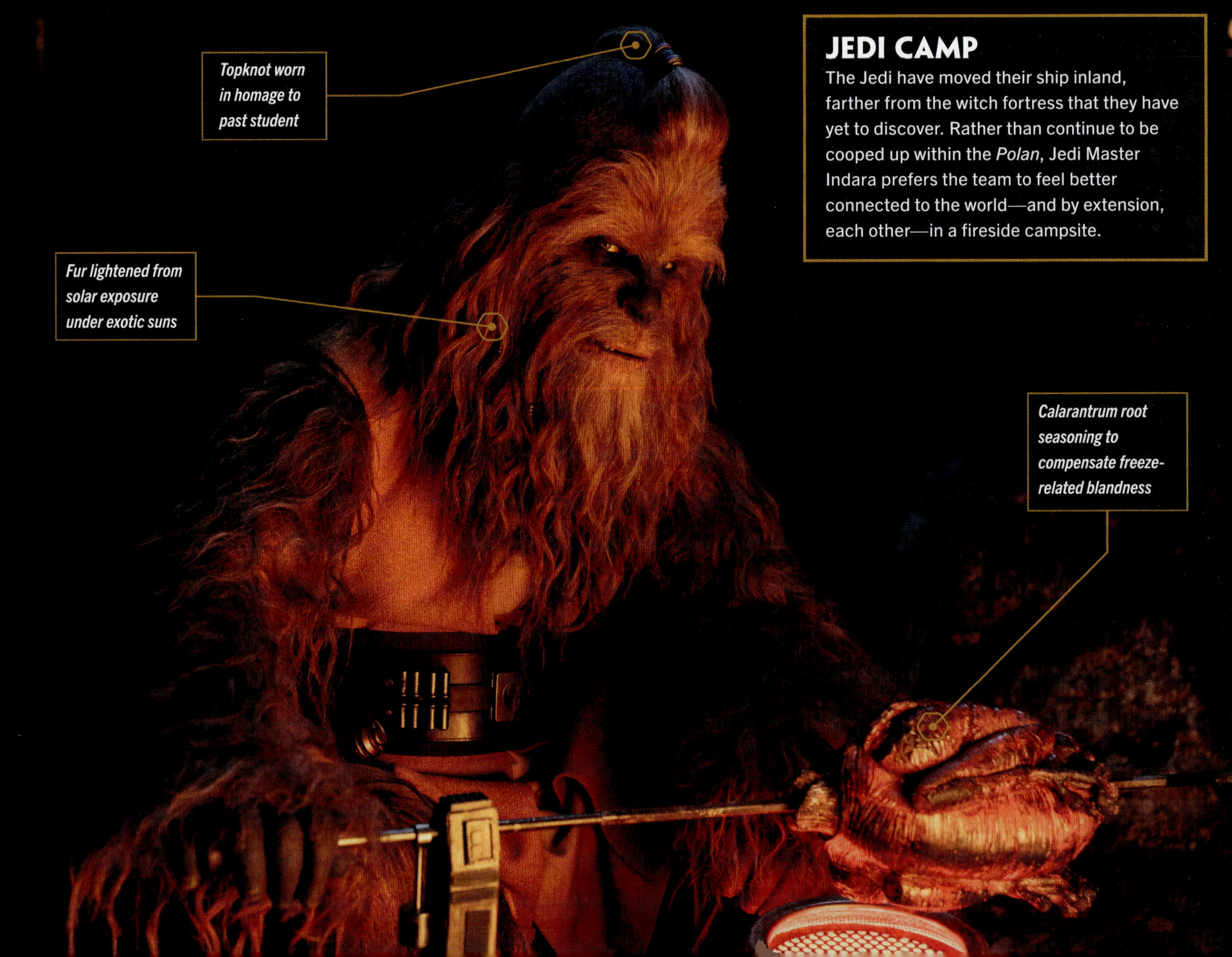

JEDI CAMP

The Jedi have moved their ship inland, farther from the witch fortress that they have yet to discover. Rather than continue to be cooped up within the *Polan*, Jedi Master Indara prefers the team to feel better connected to the world—and by extension, each other—in a fireside campsite.

Topknot worn in homage to past student

Fur lightened from solar exposure under exotic suns

Calarantrum root seasoning to compensate freeze-related blandness

INDARA

With Sol obsessing over wild theories and Torbin overcome with a sullen impatience, Indara feels that only she and Kelnacca have their attentions rightly focused.

KELNACCA

Kelnacca feels a kinship with Indara that draws him out of his reclusive shell. He cooks roast nuna legs from the ship's stores for the team.

SOL

Sol is convinced that a Force vergence on Brendok spared it from destruction and that the Jedi must seek to protect this unusual concentration of Force energy.

TORBIN

The unanswered questions regarding the vivid biosphere of Brendok have put the energetic Padawan learner, Torbin, on edge. Seven weeks of scouting and scientific analysis are gnawing away at what should be implacable Jedi patience. Indara advises him not to center on his anxieties, but Torbin cannot shake his misgivings.

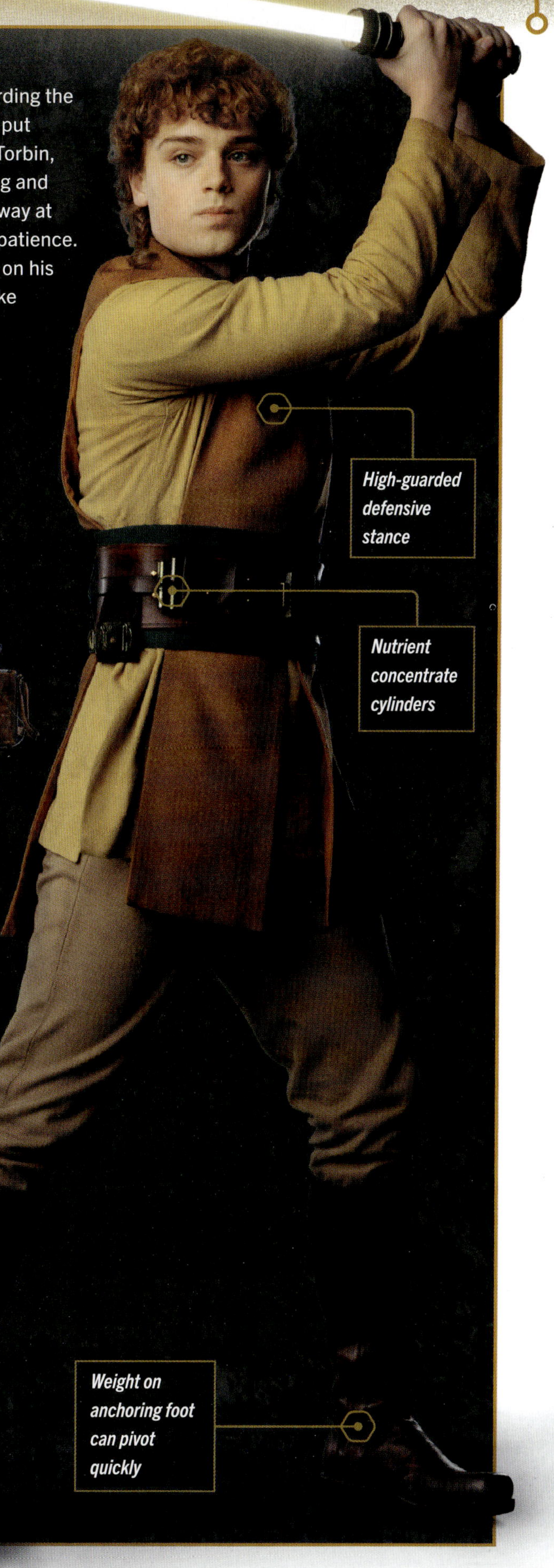

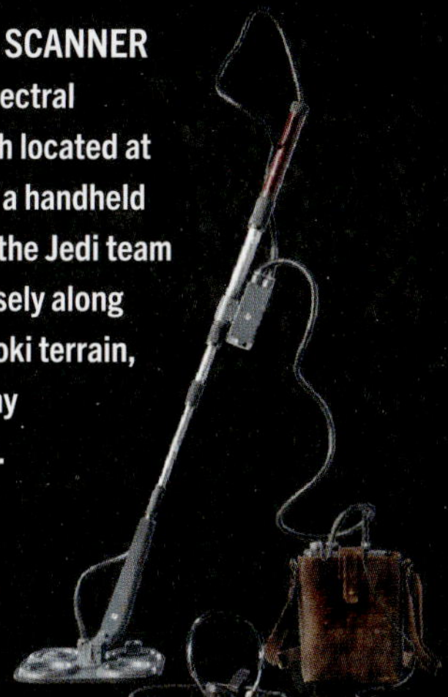

TERRAIN SCANNER
A multi-spectral sensor dish located at the end of a handheld wand lets the Jedi team sweep closely along the Brendoki terrain, seeking any anomalies.

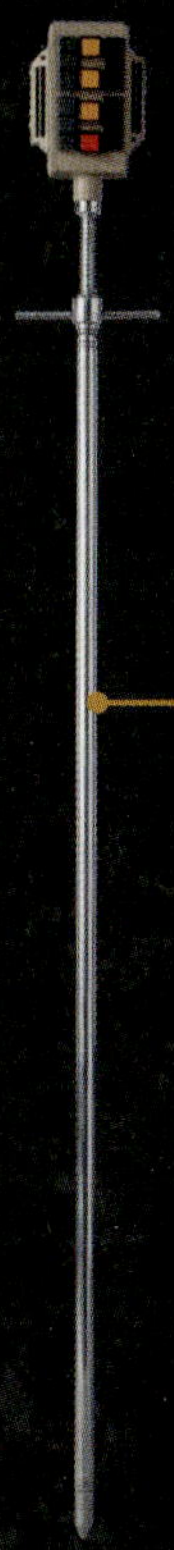

High-guarded defensive stance

Nutrient concentrate cylinders

SOIL SAMPLER
Jedi analysis of Brendoki soil samples show no detectable fallout from Cronau radiation that would be expected from the site of an Emergence.

Conductive surface to be plunged into ground

Weight on anchoring foot can pivot quickly

JEDI SPEEDER BIKES

As advanced as the sensors aboard the *Polan* are, the starship is too large, and its power consumption needs too steep, for it to function as an effective reconnaissance vehicle. For extended missions on sparsely settled worlds, ruggedized long-range speeder bikes are well suited for scouting expeditions deep in the wilderness. The Jedi team on Brendok had two such vehicles to scout the dense forests.

"WE'LL SPLIT UP THEN. SOL, FOLLOW THE RIVER. WE HAVEN'T COVERED THE NORTHLANDS YET. MEET US BACK AT THE CAMP."

MASTER INDARA TO MASTER SOL

Aft steering vanes

DATA FILE

MANUFACTURER Aratech Repulsor Company

MODEL Hussar-210 AvA

TYPE Long-range recon speeder bike

DIMENSIONS Height: 2.05 m (6 ft 8 in); Length: 4.91 m (16 ft 1 in); Width: 1.46 m (4 ft 9 in)

SPEED 500 kph (311 mph)

WEAPONS Fixed forward blaster cluster

AFFILIATION Jedi Order

REPAIR TOOLS

As defined by their mission profile, recon speeders operate far from well-stocked repair bays, so they have a ruggedized construction as well as versatile and portable tool kits to perform vital maintenance.

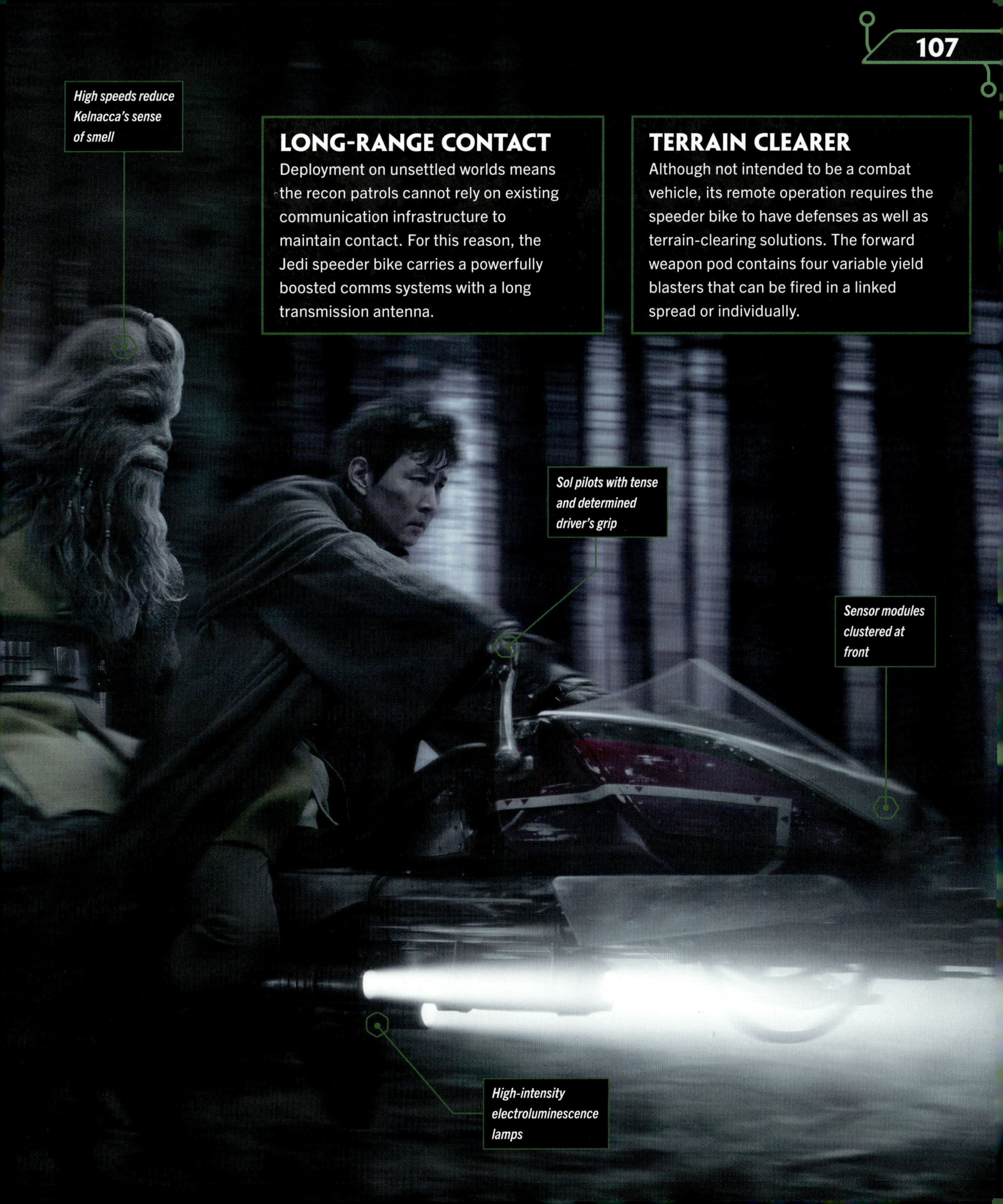

High speeds reduce Kelnacca's sense of smell

LONG-RANGE CONTACT

Deployment on unsettled worlds means the recon patrols cannot rely on existing communication infrastructure to maintain contact. For this reason, the Jedi speeder bike carries a powerfully boosted comms systems with a long transmission antenna.

TERRAIN CLEARER

Although not intended to be a combat vehicle, its remote operation requires the speeder bike to have defenses as well as terrain-clearing solutions. The forward weapon pod contains four variable yield blasters that can be fired in a linked spread or individually.

Sol pilots with tense and determined driver's grip

Sensor modules clustered at front

High-intensity electroluminescence lamps

THE TESTS

Osha's heartfelt determination to become a Jedi stirs a cautious Mother Aniseya to lower her guard. While she initially allows the testing of the girls, Aniseya advises that they lie during the examination process. Mae follows instructions, throwing the test, although the Jedi are aware of her unskilled duplicity. Osha initially tries to lie to Master Sol, but instead takes the test in good faith. Indara senses, however, that Sol is coaching the young hopeful to succeed.

Sol thinks encouraging thoughts toward Osha

Modular environment support unit

Portable conference table with integral holoprojector surface

Display screen for recorded or transmitted data

Program interface controls

Data storage unit built into handle

JEDI TESTING SCREEN

A traditional Jedi test of potential ability requires the candidate to concentrate on an unseen image and to describe it from intuition or a mental picture. At first, Osha and Mae lie about what they see.

M-COUNT RAMIFICATIONS

The results of Osha and Mae's blood tests are unexpected. The M-count is high, indicating very strong Force potential. But of greater interest is that their midi-chlorians are exact genetic duplicates, something not even identical twins typically possess. Could something unnatural be at work?

Padawan Torbin monitors activity

BLOOD SAMPLES

Another step in the testing process is the examination of a blood sample to check the M-count for levels of midi-chlorians in a candidate's bloodstream. These microbial symbionts inhabit the cells of all living beings and are a reliable marker for potential. Greater concentrations indicate greater sensitivity to the Force.

First stage respirometry sensor module

Chemically active indicator strip indicates usage

SOL'S THEORIES

Master Sol reasoned that a vergence on Brendok was responsible for its inexplicable survival from the Hyperspace Disaster. Such a vergence could be tapped to create unusual and unnatural effects in the Force by a skilled master. Sol concludes that the two girls are the results of forbidden tampering by Mother Aniseya and that they could pose a powerful danger if not properly trained.

Armored gauntlet for field missions

DISASTER

Sol's certainty that Osha and Mae are both dangerous and endangered, Torbin's impatient desire to leave Brendok, Koril's distrust of the Jedi, and the twins' intense disagreement over their futures are a disastrous combination. Fear and tempers boil out of control, and tensions explode with unintended and deadly results. This moment will shape the destinies of the survivors in the years that follow, with loss, disgrace, guilt, and vengeance rippling into the future as shock waves.

Profound shock grips young Osha

OSHA'S JOURNAL

After meeting the Jedi, Osha begins sketching out the sweeping Jedi crest seen on their belts and aboard their vessel. Her carbon-etching journal is a record of her private hopes and fears. Mae steals it in anger and sets it ablaze, causing an inferno.

KORIL VERSUS SOL

Misunderstanding Mother Aniseya's actions and abilities, Sol impales her with his lightsaber, killing the powerful witch. In her dying words, she reveals to Sol that Osha chose to follow the Jedi path. Koril is enraged by this loss and orders the scout archers to attack the Jedi, while she batters at the heartbroken Sol with her weapon.

Sol's focus is entirely on keeping Osha safe

POSSESSION

It takes the whole coven, united in incantation, to rival the abilities of the fallen Mother Aniseya. Together they ensorcell Kelnacca's mind, turning him into a raging berserker to fight his fellow Jedi. Indara intervenes and mentally cuts the Thread controlling Kelnacca. The psychic whiplash wipes out the coven, leaving the fortress strewn with bodies.

Firm handhold is a rare security in rapidly deteriorating scenario

POLAN RECOVERY BED

Osha Aniseya, believed to be the sole survivor of the witch fortress, recovers in a medical bed onboard the Jedi transport. A rejuvenative breather mask mists aerosolized bacta into her strained lungs. Only Jedi compassion can help ease her heartbreak, however.

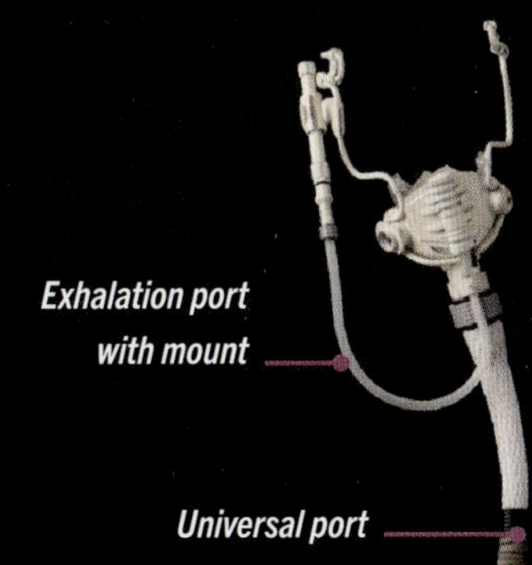

Exhalation port with mount

Universal port

Corrugated tubing leads to bacta source

CHAPTER 6

THE FINAL TARGET

The myriad threads of destiny intertwine on Brendok. Sol, the last target, brings Mae to the planet, though she escapes his grip and leads him on a frantic chase through the rings of the planet's moons. Osha follows a harrowing vision of her sister and brings the Stranger with her. Truth and resolution await in the ruins of the witch fortress.

SEEKING ANSWERS

A garbled emergency transmission from the *Polan* to Coruscant alerts Vernestra Rwoh that something terrible has happened to Sol's task force. Vernestra personally leads a small team to investigate Khofar, finding the remains of many fallen Jedi, but no trace of Sol. When his transponder beacon resurfaces on Brendok, Vernestra crews her ship with a larger group of Jedi Knights to seek answers and a resolution.

Hyperfield conductor and stabilizer coil

Deflector shield transmission plane

CANTAROS

The experimental starcutter *Cantaros* is Vernestra Rwoh's personal starship, named after her first Padawan learner. Although her piloting skills have improved considerably since her knighthood days, Vernestra still finds superluminal travel unsettling. In her youth, she would on occasion experience strange visions while meditating in hyperspace. The *Cantaros* is one of a few Jedi craft with an integrated hyperdrive system, which uses a capillary network of cooling rods in the compressed hyperfuel reservoirs to stabilize the hyperdrive between jumps.

"PREPARE A RESCUE TEAM TO DEPART FOR THE PLANET KHOFAR IMMEDIATELY."

VERNESTRA RWOH TO MOG ADANA

DATA FILE

MANUFACTURER Valkeri-Kuat Consolidated Enterprises

MODEL VKCE-7100x Starcutter

TYPE Experimental transport

DIMENSIONS Height: 8.85 m (29 ft); Length: 60.23 m (197 ft 7 in); Width: 35.17 m (115 ft 5 in)

SPEED 110 megalight per hour; Atmospheric: 1475 kph (916 mph)

WEAPONS 3 forward laser cannons; dorsal ordnance launcher (variable payload)

AFFILIATION Jedi Order

CARA MAKAMI

Skilled pilot Cara Makami is a proven ace behind the stick of a Jedi Vector. She volunteers to pilot the *Cantaros*, eager to try out the cutting-edge vessel.

Field mission under tunic

Lightsaber emits a blue blade

CANTU FALLUM

Cantu Fallum, an aquatic Dokora, has returned from negotiating a truce between warring factions on Ando, where his terse demeanor drew respect from the Aqualish.

JARIAT REGA

Newly arisen to the rank of Jedi Master, Jariat Rega has admiration for Vernestra Rwoh from studying her exploits in the Jedi archives. She aspires to impress the acclaimed Mirialan.

SAGE KINZEM

A Zinchorian, Sage Kinzem recently completed their trials to earn the rank of Jedi Knight. They are on Mog Adana's roster of effective Jedi investigators.

ESCAPE THROUGH THE RINGS

Sol sees through Mae's ruse and captures her, binding her to the medical table to allow for a moment of clear conversation once she awakens. While Mae yearns for a confession of guilt from Sol, he focuses instead on his conviction that he did right by the dangers he perceived. Mae jolts Sol with Pip's electroprod and dashes to the *Polan*'s escape craft, blasting away into Brendok's lunar rings.

Bracket socket for mechanical launch

Compressed fuel lines

Exposed P717dE ion jet engines

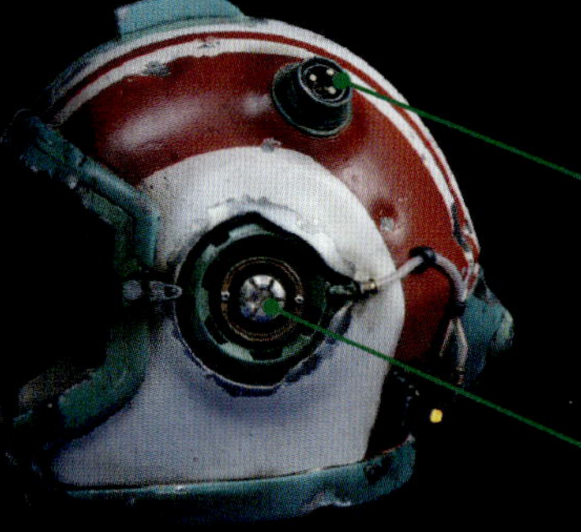

STARFIGHTER TECH

More advanced than a simple reentry pod, the *Polan's* escape craft is a full-fledged sublight and atmospheric flier with starfighter-grade maneuverability. A battered flight helmet rests inside the cockpit.

PIP RESET

To rein in Pip's independence, Mae resets the tool droid to its factory baseline. Pip's personality evaporates, and he becomes an anonymous PIP unit.

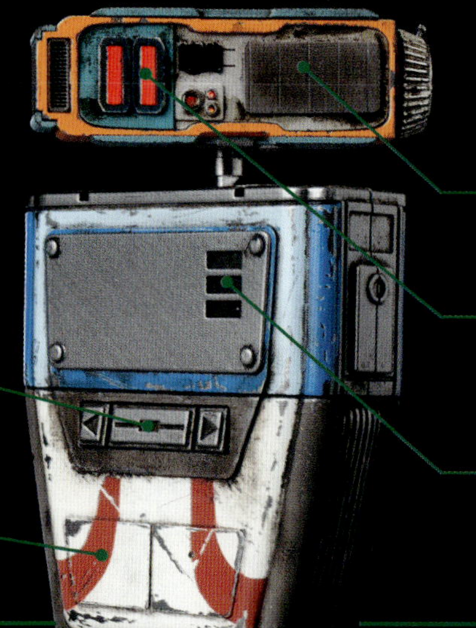

DATA FILE

MANUFACTURER Lantillian Shipwrights

MODEL P717 Finchdart

TYPE Escape craft

DIMENSIONS Height: 3.3 m (10 ft 10 in); Length: 15.6 m (51 ft 2 in); Width: 13 m (42 ft 7 in)

SPEED 100 megalight per hour; Atmospheric: 1,250 kph (777 mph)

WEAPONS None

AFFILIATION Jedi Order

AUXILIARY CRAFT

The *Finchdart* is a sleek multiuse escape and exploration craft designed as an auxiliary vessel for the *Polan*. Access to the ship is only allowed via bridge permission or emergency conditions. Once primed, the *Finchdart* drops via an accelerator cradle that launches it clear from the *Polan*.

Reinforced cockpit canopy

Navigational canard and deflector shield projector

Ramscoop collector port

The moon of Ashlasi ejects crystalline debris from its mantle via surface geysers. These fragments collect in a spectacular ring.

Though more fragile than the lumbering *Polan*, the swift *Finchdart* is available to avoid the most treacherous chunks of crystal and ice.

"SEE YOU IN HELL, JEDI."

MAE ANISEYA TO MASTER SOL

A RESOLUTION

Vernestra Rwoh follows the *Polan*'s beacon to Brendok, finding the aftermath of several confrontations, past and present. She knows firsthand how misguided intentions and incomplete information escalate into tragedy. To stem the flood of repercussions against the Jedi, she builds a dam of lies. With silent apologies to her departed friend, Vernestra holds Sol as the single party responsible for the disaster on Brendok, the string of Jedi murders, and the slaughter of Jedi on Khofar.

Closure stitched of falsehoods does not free Vernestra from the burden of the past

THE BLEEDING OF KYBER

As Osha hears Sol's confession of killing her mother, a rage grows within her. Her fist clenches on Sol's broken lightsaber, her skin coming in direct contact with its exposed kyber crystal. Such dark anger physically alters the crystal, bleeding it so that the blade emerges a brilliant red.

A CLEAN SLATE

Escaping the Jedi, Osha forges a deal with the Stranger. He will free Mae from his vendetta by wiping her memory of their presence, ridding her of deadly secrets. In exchange, Osha commits to the Stranger, vowing to become his acolyte.

A NEW BOND

Osha Aniseya has turned her back on the Jedi Order, stung by the secrets kept throughout her time with them. She is drawn to the Stranger for his apparent honesty in his offer of power, and for a kinship found in those betrayed by mentors.

Torch to ignite the traditional funeral pyre reserved for Jedi Masters

A FALLEN APPRENTICE

In Vernestra's long life, she's had multiple apprentices. One student eclipses the rest in a shadow of regret: a student that fell to the temptations of the dark side, resulting in conflict and heartbreak. She had thought that matter closed, but the presence of the Stranger on Brendok is hauntingly familiar.

THE SENATE

The Galactic Senate is the primary governing body of the Republic. It consists of hundreds of representatives who have a democratic voice in determining the Republic's laws and policies. Some senators represent individual worlds, while others speak for whole sectors or blocs of worlds to balance out population and influence. Just how an individual senator is promoted to such a position is determined by their local customs, but some degree of senatorial presence is a right that comes with Republic membership.

Over centuries of uninterrupted harmonious rule, procedures and policies meant to clarify and guide the governing process have grown into a sprawling bureaucracy. Within these layers of cumbersome protocols, clever and ambitious senators can find exploitable loopholes and mechanisms to tie up legislation, accelerate graft, or hide misconduct.

The zenith of the High Republic, when much of the Senate's rule was benevolent, has not long passed. But decay and cynicism has begun to set seed, and narrow interests that are disconnected from the greater good have found ways to influence the future.

CHANCELLOR VEETH DRELLIK

Supreme Chancellor Veeth Drellik gives the benefit of the doubt to the Jedi Order and has come to rely on Vernestra Rwoh's candor. Still, he gives time to Rayencourt's concerns and convenes a formal tribunal to review the situation.

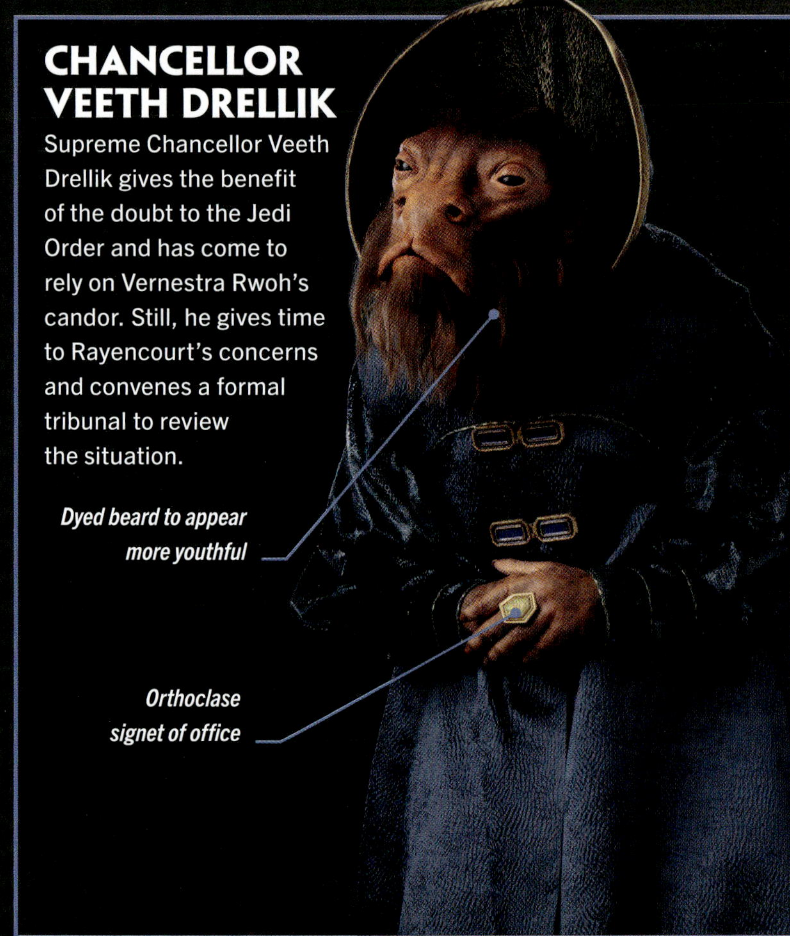

Dyed beard to appear more youthful

Orthoclase signet of office

SENATOR ISEDWA CHUWANT

A representative of Abednedo, Senator Isedwa Chuwant is an ally to Vernestra Rwoh and surreptitiously provides feedback into Senate gossip that incriminates the Jedi Order. Chuwant especially distrusts Rayencourt and wishes to ensure his politicking doesn't overly impact the Jedi Order's ability to operate.

SENATOR WORUS RAYENCOURT

Senator Worus Rayencourt, of the Thusa sector, is an advocate for stricter senatorial supervision of the Jedi Order. He pushes for the chancellor to convene a special tribunal with the Jedi liaison to the Senate, Master Vernestra Rwoh.

SENATOR AXUT KLEM

Swayed to Rayencourt's position, Senator Axut Klem has begun to echo his contentious talking points. Though the stern Praelion has few direct dealings with the Jedi Order, Klem is an influential leader of the Japrael sector. It houses two Jedi outposts, which he is willing to surveil.

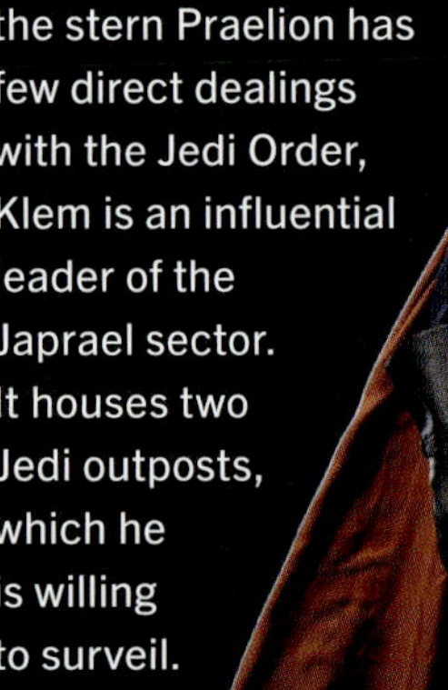

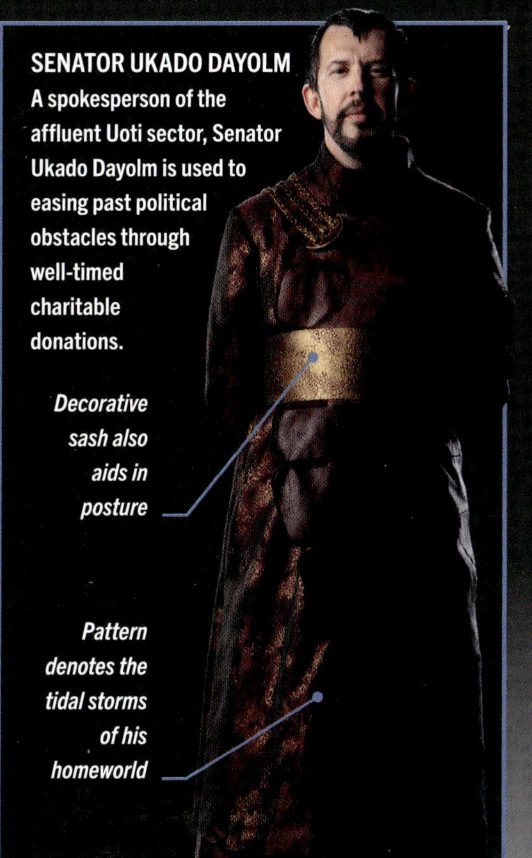

SENATOR UKADO DAYOLM
A spokesperson of the affluent Uoti sector, Senator Ukado Dayolm is used to easing past political obstacles through well-timed charitable donations.

Decorative sash also aids in posture

Pattern denotes the tidal storms of his homeworld

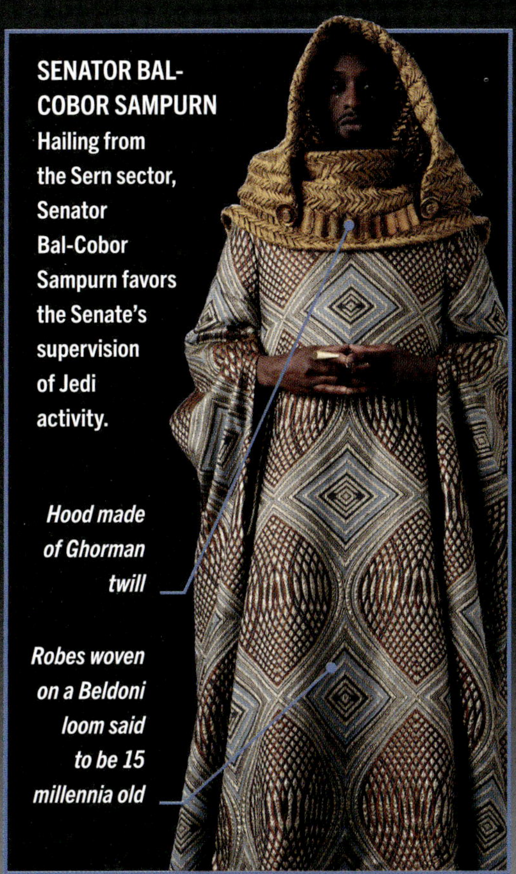

SENATOR BAL-COBOR SAMPURN
Hailing from the Sern sector, Senator Bal-Cobor Sampurn favors the Senate's supervision of Jedi activity.

Hood made of Ghorman twill

Robes woven on a Beldoni loom said to be 15 millennia old

SENATOR JOMANDI GRILAO
Senator Jomandi Grilao represents the Droma sector. She wishes to bolster the authority of the Judiciary.

Heir rings indicate children

Pattern of the Lonnawi assembly

SENATOR AVALU PORVIRAN
From the Bormea sector, Senator Porviran keeps an open mind during the tribunal.

Decorative disk also serves as data recorder

Beaded Ganthelan fabric

SENATOR SAHEN IDANE
Long an ally to the Jedi, Senator Idane represents the Chommell sector and has close ties with the elected Naboo royalty.

Belt sash a gift from Queen Yovité

Fabric of Theed finery

SENATOR OONLI CHARUM
Senator Charum is an envoy from the Sumitra sector, neighbor to Rayencourt's, and is often in step with his views.

Braids honor constituent world Thustra

UNCERTAINTY LIES AHEAD

The dark side by its very nature is hard to see. Vernestra cagily distracts the senators by placing the blame for the recent tragedies on Sol's transgressions, but it is a most uncomfortable lie. The return of her long-lost student is not something she can so easily obscure. She seeks counsel from the Order's wisest.

INDEX

Page numbers in **bold** refer to main entries.

OLEGA CITY VENDOR TOY RANCOR

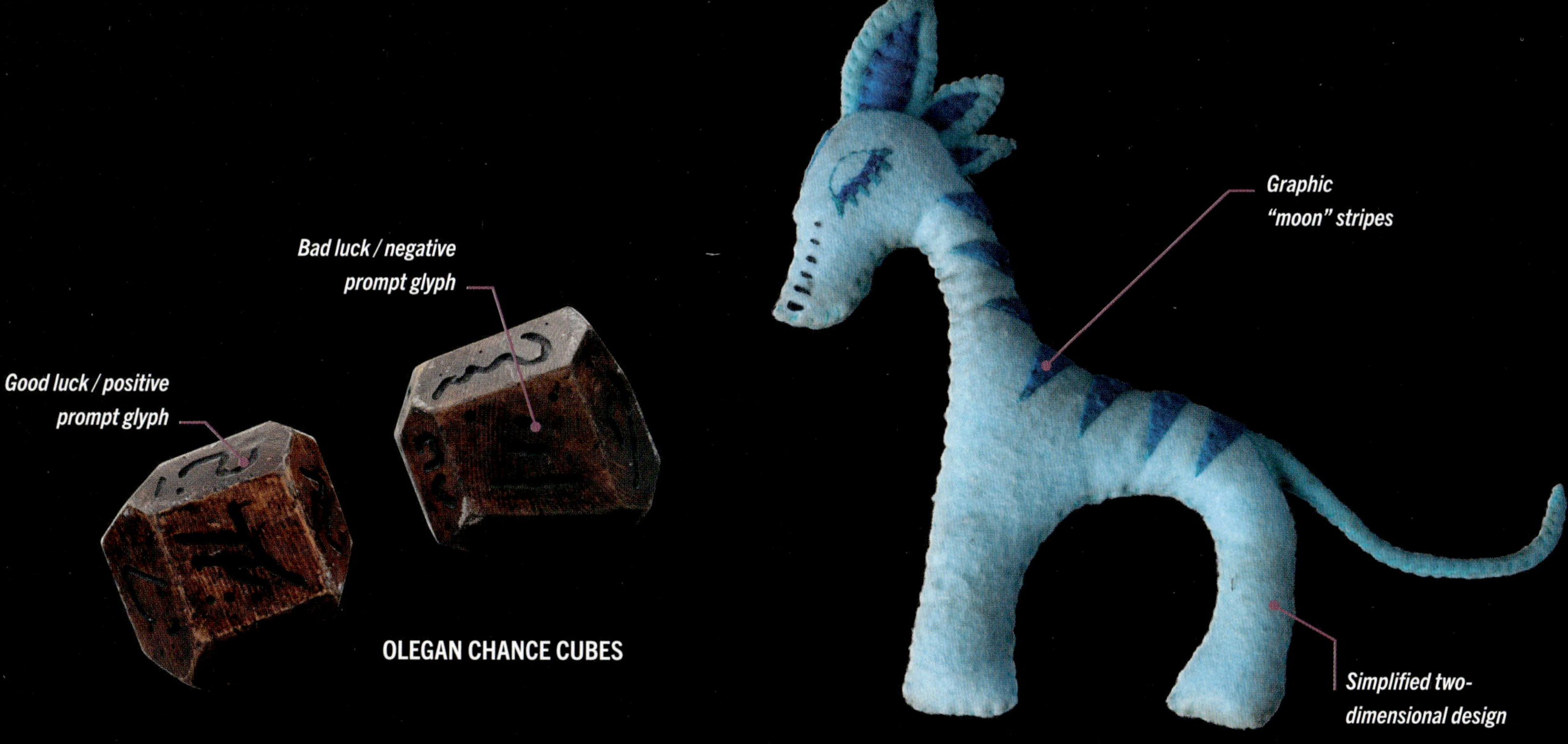

OLEGAN CHANCE CUBES

OSHA'S TARANDOX TODDLER TOY

Senior Editor Matt Jones
US Senior Editor Jennette ElNaggar
Project Art Editor Chris Gould
Production Editor Marc Staples
Senior Production Controller Laura Andrews
Managing Editor Emma Grange
Managing Art Editor Vicky Short
Publisher Paula Regan
Art Director Charlotte Coulais
Publishing Director Mark Searle

Designed and edited for DK by XAB Design

FOR LUCASFILM
Senior Editor Brett Rector
Creative Director Michael Siglain
Art Director Troy Alders
Concept Artists Jon McCoy, David Dobbins, Thang Le, Ralph McQuarrie, Erik Tiemens, and Andrée Wallin
Asset Group Chris Argyropoulos, Allison Bird, Jackey Cabrera, Elinor De La Torre, Gabrielle Levenson, Nick Miano, Bryce Pinkos, and Sarah Williams
Story Group Leland Chee, Kate Izquierdo, Matt Martin, and Phil Szostak

First published in Great Britain in 2025 by
Dorling Kindersley Limited
20 Vauxhall Bridge Road,
London SW1V 2SA

The authorised representative in the EEA is
Dorling Kindersley Verlag GmbH. Arnulfstr. 124,
80636 Munich, Germany

A Penguin Random House Company
10 9 8 7 6 5 4 3 2 1
001–344432–June/2025

A CIP catalogue record for this book
is available from the British Library.
ISBN: 978-0-2417-1042-5

Printed and bound in China

www.dk.com
www.starwars.com

MIX
Paper | Supporting responsible forestry
FSC™ C018179
www.fsc.org

This book was made with Forest Stewardship Council™ certified paper – one small step in DK's commitment to a sustainable future. Learn more at **www.dk.com/uk/information/sustainability**

ACKNOWLEDGMENTS

Pablo Hidalgo: I am grateful to Leslye Headland and Rayne Roberts for their generous access throughout the development, production, and postproduction of this wonderful series. Getting direct interaction with department heads like Kevin Jenkins, Jennifer Bryan, Neal Scanlan, and Katie Newitt ensures that all the detailed work of their teams can shine in a book like this. Thanks to Jeff King, Jason McCallef, Mog McIntyre, Alex Hayes, Byron Ross, and Gemma Yianni for their invaluable help.

Special thanks to Julian Foddy for VFX insights, and for creating the custom render of a noodle-serving droid that can be found in these pages. Amandla, thank you for the thoughtfulness in all you do, and for some great questions and answers about the Force's deepest mysteries.

Thanks again to DK, Michael Siglain, and James Waugh for the continued opportunities. Thanks to the Lucasfilm Business Affairs team for lightsabering through some stubborn red tape.

Thank you to Kristen for your love and support and for watching *The Acolyte* together.

To those who have been celebrating Light and Life since the start of this era, this is for you. We are all the Republic.

DK Publishing: DK would like to thank Pablo Hidalgo for his contributions to the book; Jason Fry and Christopher Ibbitt for their contributions to the galaxy map; XAB Design for their work on the book; and Chelsea Alon at Disney.

Stun blaster holster comfortably draped

The ever-attentive Pip, ready to help